the new Convict Code

Other Works by Kit Cummings

Peace Behind the Wire:
A Nonviolent Resolution

Protect the Dream:
40 Days of Power

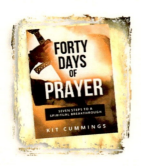

Forty Days of Prayer:
Seven Steps to a
Spiritual Breakthrough

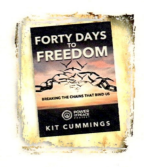

Forty Days to Freedom:
Breaking the Chains That Bind Us

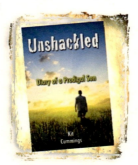

Unshackled:
Diary of a Prodigal Son

the new Convict Code

BRINGING PEACE TO THE STREETS
FROM BEHIND THE WIRE

KIT CUMMINGS

BOOKLOGIX®
Alpharetta, GA

The author has tried to recreate events, locations, and conversations from his memories of them. In some instances, in order to maintain their anonymity, the author has changed the names of individuals and places. He may also have changed some identifying characteristics and details such as physical attributes, occupations, and places of residence.

Copyright © 2021 by Kit Cummings

All rights reserved. No part of this book may be reproduced or transmitted in any form or by any means, electronic or mechanical, including photocopying, recording, or any information storage and retrieval system, without permission in writing from the publisher. For more information, address BookLogix, c/o Permissions Department, 1264 Old Alpharetta Rd., Alpharetta, GA 30005.

ISBN: 978-1-6653-0012-4 - Paperback
eISBN: 978-1-6653-0013-1 - ePub
eISBN: 978-1-6653-0014-8 - mobi

Library of Congress Control Number: 2021900319

Printed in the United States of America   0 2 0 8 2 1

⊚This paper meets the requirements of ANSI/NISO Z39.48-1992 (Permanence of Paper)

Author photo by Justin Jarrell

*This book is dedicated to Terrie—
my wife, my soulmate,
my loyal partner, and my best friend.
Without your love, encouragement, and constant support,
I could not do the things that God has called me to do
or be the man that He created me to be.
All my love forever.*

*Darkness cannot drive out darkness, only light can do that.
Hatred cannot drive out hatred, only love can do that.*
—Dr. Martin Luther King Jr.

Contents

Foreword		xi
Introduction		xiii
Act One	**The Influence of Sir Brown**	**1**
Chapter One	The Story of POPP	3
Chapter Two	Violence Is Not the Answer	17
Chapter Three	The Seven POPP Principles	31
Act Two	**The Story of Roots**	**69**
Chapter Four	Where Are the Dreamers?	73
Chapter Five	The Antivirus	81
Chapter Six	The Convict Code	91
Chapter Seven	The New POPP Code	107
Chapter Eight	Punishment vs. Reward	125
Act Three	**Chewy's Redemption**	**147**
Chapter Nine	The Dark Side Is Organized	153
Chapter Ten	The Incarcerated Mind	165
Chapter Eleven	The Mental Battlefield	177
Chapter Twelve	A Solitary Life	191
Act Four	**Modern-Day Heroes**	**199**
Chapter Thirteen	Violence and a Young Generation	205
Chapter Fourteen	Young Men Need Strong Men	217
Chapter Fifteen	Regarding White Privilege	229
Chapter Sixteen	A Forgotten City Remembered	239
Conclusion		257
Acknowledgments		263
Bibliography		265

Foreword

Peace was on the move at the facility where I currently reside, but little fires kept popping up—fires meaning beefs and strong misunderstandings that kept leading to violence. A few powerful and influential brothers would get together and douse the flames before they spread into an uncontrollable wildfire, but we just couldn't quench the fires quick enough before another burst out of nowhere. Then we were told the Power of Peace Project (POPP) was coming to our prison. Not many understood what it was, and most didn't want any part of it. Then we gathered and were able to experience POPP. I know magic attracts magic, good finds good, and our forty-day journey had begun. There was laughter, tears, pain, sadness, confusion, and inspiration, all shared by dudes who rarely even spoke to each other.

From day one, commitments were made to attempt peaceful resolutions. Miracles began to take place. Then he was gone, and it was time for us to own it for ourselves. Sometimes the message can be just as powerful, or even more powerful, than the messenger. We never personally met Mahatma Gandhi, Dr. Martin Luther King Jr., or Malcolm X, but their messages live on just the same. It was like that for us with Kit. His methods and principles are applied, and wars are averted, relationships are built, dialogue develops, and finding peaceful solutions is the new way. He distributes wristbands, and they read: "Hope Is the New

Dope." Wearing these bands forges bonds. They've become conversation starters, and they remind the wearer of the oath they took to get along and to find peaceful alternatives. Peace is definitely on the move behind the wire, and we're gathering momentum every day.

We are the Power of Peace.

—Sir Brown
A Brother Behind the Wire

Introduction

It's 2008, and I am desperately trying to find my voice. I had preached and preached for fifteen years, and then I just ran out of things to say. What does a preacher do when he's lost his heart? For several years I bounced around from one thing to another after my dream crashed and I fell out of full-time ministry. Nothing did it for me; nothing made that inner bell go off like it did when I was in front of an audience. Those crowds are intoxicating, even addictive.

Preaching and teaching is without a doubt what I was born to do, and I was called to it as a young man in 1990. However, after much ministry success, I simply ran out of gas, stumbled, and fell hard. My struggle with alcohol and drugs stole my dream, and I hit rock bottom in 2004. Divorce, rehab, and bankruptcy turned my whole world upside down, and this time it was *live* for everyone to see. I had gone from a popular, powerful preacher to a cautionary tale.

I took my last drink in 2005, and everything began to change. Sober and resolute, I set out to find my heart. With fear and trepidation, I began to preach again, but I had no idea what God had in store for me. Then the catalyst I needed arrived. A good friend of mine gave me the best ministry assignment I had ever received. He said, "Go out into the world and see what God is up to and come back and tell us." That simple charge changed my life. I set out to discover where God is working the most powerfully, and I haven't stopped since.

I began with a homeless mission in Downtown Atlanta. That led me to work with at-risk youth in the schools. From there I went into a jail and started working with a high-profile gang member, which led me into the prison system working to bring rival gangs together. This became my crazy dream. Ever since I received that challenge years ago, I have been in over one hundred prisons, jails, detention centers, and rehab facilities, and worked with over ten thousand inmates and residents. I've been in dozens of schools and worked with thousands of teens as well. Over the course of my career, I've definitely put in the ten thousand hours it takes to master one's craft. It turns out "what God was up to" was in places that few ever see.

There is darkness and light behind that razor wire. There are heroes and monsters behind those walls. There is tragedy and redemption in these hopeless places. I began to witness it, study it, master it, and attempt to change it. Nobody has ever seen the best work of my life except those beautiful and brilliant convicts dressed in all the different colors of the US prison-industrial complex. The two million men locked up in the Land of the Free became my congregation, and those dirty tables became my pulpit. It became my safe place, because they didn't judge me. I shared things with them that I wouldn't tell anyone else. The things I needed to talk about aren't things you can speak about in church. What I needed was catharsis. I could be free and absolutely me behind that wire. They adopted me, and now I'm a made man. They guarded me, protected me, taught me, and redeemed me. I owe them everything, because God used them to help this drunken, fallen preacher find his way home. This misfit band of brothers on the road to redemption became the family—and the unlikely congregation—I so desperately needed.

I learned that sometimes you can trust imprisoned men more than free men. Inside all of these prisons, there is something they call the "convict code." It's a way of life, with rules of engagement and a mode of operation. It's not a matter of if you decide to play, but how fast you can learn the game and play it well. There are no exceptions to the rules, and there are severe consequences for violations. The ones who run things have earned their place and paid their dues. If you decide to affiliate with a criminal organization for protection, there are no do-overs; it's a decision you make for life. Life is unpredictable there, but the convict code is something you can count on.

What if people in the free world lived by a standard code with defined ways to deal with conflict, transgressions, and disagreements? What if everyone knew the consequences for their actions before they made a move? We live in a world with less and less accountability for our personal decisions. That is not a convict's world. I reasoned that if we could change the convict code, then we could change the prison system, and that's what I've been attempting to do for many years now. We're simply changing the rules of the game and revising the code. If prisoners can instead develop a new code around respect, integrity, loyalty, and honor on the chain gang, as they call it, then maybe we can shift prison culture and bring about true reform.

The world is in dire need of solutions. We keep these men and women locked away in hellholes that we build in the middle of nowhere. These facilities house the hated, feared, and forgotten. I have believed for some time that God will raise up an army of freedom fighters from behind the wire to come home and clean up our streets, to come home and lead the young who have lost their way. If we provide them with the motivation to change and the tools to carry it out, and they receive spiritual power from above, then together we can create the solutions we so desperately need. This book is about that journey and the solutions I have found hiding in a place no one dares to look.

I need to say one more thing before we begin. I know these men have done terrible things and caused untold suffering. I know we can never get back all the things they have stolen or repair the lives they have ruined forever. However, someone has to love them, someone has to believe in them, and someone has to help them, before they are released back into our communities only to reoffend and continue hurting the ones we love. I've been affected by their crimes personally, and through them I am making my "living amends" for the mistakes I have made as well. This is my commitment to you: We'll do our best to help them heal, find a better way, and come home as an army of "returning citizens" to fix up what they tore up.

While I will mainly be speaking about incarcerated men and solutions to decrease violence in adult male and juvenile facilities, these principles most definitely work in women's facilities as well. Deep down, everyone wants peace. We're built for it.

This book is divided into four acts. Each act will begin with one of the heroes who came into my life and changed it forever. In Act One we will look at the history of the Power of Peace Project, why we need it, how it works, and the principles that make it so effective. Let us begin.

The POPP Sisters at the Nebraska State Prison for Women

Act One

THE INFLUENCE OF SIR BROWN

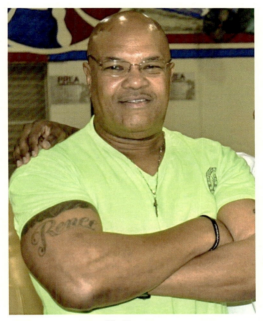

Sir Brown

My best friend behind the wire, out of all the thousands of prisoners I've been in front of, is a man they call "Sir Brown." He is the closest thing I've found to an emerging Gandhi, King, or Mandela in the US prison system. He's not affiliated with any criminal organization, but gang leaders come to him for counsel. When violence is brewing, Sir Brown is the one the warden sends for. He's stopped countless fights, put down potential riots, and helped so many inmates learn a better way to live and how to resolve conflict peacefully. When gangs are about to go to war, Sir Brown deescalates. It's an amazing thing to see.

He's a poet, a singer, an athlete, and a mentor. He's one of the strongest men I've ever known mentally, physically, emotionally, or spiritually. He is incredibly valuable to wardens and staff in every prison he resides in. When Sir Brown is in the general population, regardless of the prison, there will be less violence, period. I know he has bad days, but in all the years I've known him, I've never heard him gripe or complain, not even once. He is my friend, my brother, my counselor, my consigliere, and many times, my bodyguard. While doing a life sentence he has completed almost every program the state offers. I believe the free world needs his voice, his wisdom, and the solutions we have found together behind the wire.

I pray for him daily and fully believe a pro bono defense attorney will appear and appeal his case, as it appears to have many holes. Prisons need more and more men of his caliber to rise up and reform this broken system. Give me an army of "Sir Browns" and we could turn this whole thing upside down. There would be no Power of Peace Project if Sir Brown hadn't helped me lay the foundation.

At this very moment, with the race riots in the streets, and when it is open season on "white boys" behind the wire, his prison is one of the only ones in my state seeing little, if any, racial violence. Our methods and the ones POPP employ can work on the streets as well, but it will take humility for the system to utilize prisoners to bring about peace. Who better to help bring about reform than those on the front lines?

Throughout this book I will highlight some of Sir Brown's wisdom in his own words. I love this brother, and I am committed to setting him free. He is one of the most brilliant brothers I've ever met, and he inspires me to be a better man.

Chapter One
THE STORY OF POPP

The Original POPP Squad

On January 18, 2011, twelve men inside Georgia's most violent and dangerous prison signed a pledge and set into motion a peace movement that would spread to prisons across the country and even down into Mexico. We didn't know what we were doing; they were just cautious dreamers and men who were sick and tired of living in hell. They believed they could make a difference, and they made a dangerous decision to dream again. They took a solemn oath to follow iconic peacemakers from around the world and to practice nonviolence for forty days. They didn't think it was possible—not in this prison, which has more active gang members than any other prison in the state; not in this prison, where 80 percent of the inmates are doing fifteen years or more; not in this prison, where a third of the inmates are considered mental-health cases. But they dared to believe because they simply wanted a better quality of life.

I didn't know these new friends and brothers were about to change my life. We went to work and created the seven steps to peace. Every week, we met to design a new code of conduct among the convicts. It was edgy and dangerous, as they were about to put themselves out front in a place where you don't do that. But this appealed to these tough men who were desperate to change their lives. The warden hadn't given me permission to try it, though he said I could teach it in my weekly class, so I told the men to keep it to themselves. However, they couldn't keep this secret, and soon the word began to spread. Good news is like that. Soon these brothers were bringing men to me on the yard, and they vouched for me and for one another. More leaders wanted in. Gang leaders sent for me, and we explained what it was and why we were doing it. The warden got on board because he couldn't contain it any longer. He gave us the visitation room on Fridays and allowed an open call for anyone who wanted to come to what we called "Forty Days of Peace." Soon the room was filled with many of the most influential men on the compound.

Something was happening, and it was palpable. The energy in this prison was shifting, and there was less and less violence. There were no stabbings for thirty days in a row, which hadn't happened there in a very long time. The warden allowed me to choose a group of about fifteen "men of influence," and we met on Friday mornings in the small chapel for our POPP leadership meeting before our larger gathering. We discussed issues, conflicts, and potential problems between gangs. We negotiated peace between the rivals, and they began calling different shots. Riots were put down, hits were called off, and assaults on officers and inmates declined rapidly. Soon there was so little violence that it got the attention of the state, and this prison won Institution of the Year in the State of Georgia, something it had never done in the twenty-two years since it had opened. We were on the map.

I had no idea if it could be scaled or replicated—maybe we had just caught lightning in a bottle, and it was a unique, once-in-a-lifetime miracle. I soon found out the same magic happened wherever we took it. It spread to the Midwest and then out west, and then across the border into a Mexican prison where we saw cartel rivals work together to bring about peace. I wondered if it would work with juvenile offenders too, and it did. We saw amazing results in three juvenile prisons in Ohio, which experienced outcomes they hadn't seen prior to POPP. But could it work with tough kids in the free world? Again, we found that it could and it would, if we practiced the same principles we developed with the men behind the wire.

The kids saw this as cool because it was "hip-hop gangster." Unlikely role models began to emerge, men who spoke their language with a new message. So, we took POPP into inner-city schools, where kids were hitting the streets, joining gangs, and lining up to go to prison. Then I got called to the suburbs, where kids were dying from overdose, suicide, and accidental death, and it worked there too. "Hope Is the New Dope" became our mantra, and I continued going wherever I was invited. It's been a wild ride over the years as POPP has impacted thousands of inmates and kids, and given hope to those who lost it.

So now the question is this: Can POPP work in the current political climate where the streets are on fire and there's no hope in sight? I'm crazy enough to believe it can. This book is about solutions that prisoners have implemented to change their world, and their methods are primed to be the medicine the streets so desperately need.

Mass Incarceration in the Land of the Free

In 1970, there were approximately two hundred thousand inmates in the US prison-industrial complex. Just thirty years later, there were over two million. This didn't happen by accident; it was systematic. Today in this country we are spending considerably more on prisons than schools. For the first time in our nation's history, over half of prisoners are twenty-five years old or younger. One-third go in for nonviolent crimes, but over two-thirds are released after having become violent. Two-thirds reoffend or get revoked, and go back to prison within three years of their release. More and more prisons are becoming privatized, as they are being bought from the state by big corporations. These corporations sign contracts with the state guaranteeing that at least 85 percent of the beds will remain full at all times, which incentivizes them to lock up more and more fathers, brothers, and sons.

Mandatory minimums and three-strike laws lead to inmates doing longer time for lesser crimes. Privatization is now reaching paroles and probations as well, which gives the powers-that-be the authority to send ex-offenders back to prison at will, as they hold the keys. Prisoners produce goods for the free market while being paid as little as ten cents an hour for their labor, and in my home state of Georgia they don't get paid a thing. This equates to slave labor. Poor healthcare and very little mental-health treatment set them up to be poorly prepared for the free world if and when they get out. Upon release, returning citizens now have a felony record that follows them wherever they go, which limits their ability to secure decent housing and a steady job, which only increases the chances of them going back to prison.

The US has only 5 percent of the world's population, but locks up 25 percent of the world's incarcerated. Make no mistake, we have made corrections into big business, a business that spends $80 billion a year. The correctional system creates tremendous profit, so those who run it are not incentivized to change it. Why would they? It works for them just as Jim Crow laws worked for the racist South, until Dr. King carefully dismantled it by arousing the conscience of a sleeping nation. And he did so with nonviolence. The oppressor will never give up their unjust system until public opinion changes and they are forced to come to the table. In the same way the nation had to watch the horrors in Selma and Birmingham in order to be compelled to act, the country now needs to see what's going on behind the wire before they will care. I believe they will.

Right now, the world shouts about police brutality and systemic racism, but no one is talking about what's been going on behind prison walls for decades. These are the front lines of police brutality. These are the front lines of systemic racism. It's time to shine a light on the 2.3 million souls locked up in the Land of the Free. What if it were your father or son? They are *all* somebody's family, and studies say as many as one out of twenty are not guilty for the crime they were convicted of. What if it were your mom, or daughter—would you care then? It's time to find our compassion for those thrown into a system where true rehabilitation is a pipe dream.

A Broken System Built to Fail

Imagine you have an eighteen-year-old son. He goes to a party and starts hanging out with some "cool guys" that he doesn't know very well. They ask him if he wants to go with them to another party. These are bad boys, but he is enticed. They stop at a liquor store to get more beer and one of them says he's going to get some easy money. Your son is nervous and stays in the car while they all go inside. All of a sudden the boys run out, jump in the car, and speed off. Your son doesn't know that one of them has a gun. As they speed through a red light, a cop pulls them over just as the call goes out about the liquor store robbery. All four are arrested and charged.

Your family doesn't have the money to bond him out, so there he sits. In your county, the court system is backed up, and your son won't have his time before the judge for approximately nine months. You also can't afford legal representation, so you have to settle for a public defender. Your attorney has a hundred other cases and is grossly overworked and underpaid. When she does have time to work on your son's case, the main goal is to get a plea deal, as 80–90 percent of these cases are never even going to trial.

Here's where the game changes. The prosecuting attorney says the other boys have agreed to cooperate, and they say your son came up with the idea. He threatens ten years on the armed robbery charge, but says your son will be home in five. They have a strong case and warn you that you'll lose if it goes to trial, and he will get more time. As he sits day after day, the pressure becomes too much to bear, so you decide to take the deal. Once inside, he does what he has to do for protection and gets caught up in the gang life, which will continue on the streets upon his release. Your heart is broken as you wonder what just happened. We've lost another young one to a broken system.

What do you do? This is a very real scenario happening in communities all over the country. If the majority of cases went to trial, as our judicial system was designed, the courts would be overwhelmed, and the system would shut down. This is a broken business model built to fail, and young people are fueling it with more and more "customers."

I Love Going to Prison

When I tell people I love going to prison, they think I'm crazy. Maybe I am. I mean it, though; there's almost nowhere else I'd rather be. Of course, I go in through the front gate, I've never had to change my clothes, and I get to leave whenever I want to! But I absolutely love working with the men in a maximum-security prison—the tougher, the better. People often tilt their head and make a strange expression when I say that. And then they ask *why*. You see, for most people prison is the last place they would want to visit. That's because they see the violence, the danger, and the darkness on TV and in the movies. But that's exactly why I love it so much. I see peace in the violence, hope in the danger, and light in the darkness. Prison is a place of such contrasts. Peace, hope, and light shine so bright because those things are so rare behind the wire.

If I had to choose one thing I'm hooked on about prison work (and yes, it's an addiction for me, as I get hooked on whatever makes me feel good), it would have to be the love and gratitude I witness spilling out of their eyes, the hardest and toughest eyes on the planet. They can't keep it to themselves. They come in looking so hard and tough and angry, and then I wait for it. As I speak, and they listen, I know it's coming. Then I see it. First, they're sitting back in their chairs. They begin to straighten up, and they lean in with their elbows on their knees. When they realize they're talking to their neighbor, they shut up. They try not to laugh at my jokes, but they slip. They try not to make eye contact, but they can't look away. And then I wait for them to break into applause on their own. At this point I know I've got 'em. Their eyes tell the whole story as they begin to laugh freely, and maybe even shed a tear. That's when I know they've let me in once again. It turns out they're not so hard after all.

I've tried to explain what it's like to someone who's never preached behind the wire. It's not like they're hungry in a spiritual sense, because hunger means you want more. It's more like they have an insatiable thirst, like, "If I don't get some of that water, I'm going to die." You see the desperation in their eyes, as it's been so long since they've had anyone pour into them. Sure, they get revival preachers every now and then trying to save their souls. They get well-meaning counselors, chaplains, and teachers trying to help them, but many don't even show up anymore. They have settled for less than enough. The world has told them they're worthless for so long, they eventually believe it. So, when they sit there in that hopeless condition, and I offer them some cool water, they jump right in. That's the magic I seek behind the wire. I am hooked on it: Hope Is the New Dope.

Unlikely Role Models

I have been telling these men behind the wire for years that they would become role models someday. They laugh at me and roll their eyes, saying they've never been called role models. The truth is we are all role models to those who are watching us. Whether it be our kids, our friends and family, our coworkers, or fellow congregants, we are constantly modeling behavior to others. But I meant what they thought I meant, that one day they would be positive role models for this young generation.

Young people need inspiring role models now more than ever. They glorify the millionaire athlete, who gets convicted of rape. They idolize the millionaire rapper, who gets convicted of aggravated assault. They glorify the millionaire movie starlet, who dies of a drug overdose. They idolize the millionaire politician, who supposedly stands for them, who gets convicted of a hate crime himself. So, where are the role models today? Maybe we're looking in all the wrong places.

They Can Show Us the Way

The incarcerated want to change as badly as anybody does, but they have believed the lie that they cannot change. Nobody believes they even want to, much less that they are capable. What they desperately need is hope, so we insert that magical and missing component. Hope is a dangerous thing in a prison, because they have had it snatched away so many times. They want hope, but they fear it. I have found that adding this elixir to a hopeless situation has the power to change everything.

Think about it—they have already proven that they are willing to do whatever it takes to get what they want. We just need to redirect their desires. They have already proven that they can walk into hell and figure out a way to survive. We just have to show them a new type of courage. They have already proven that they can use their influence to persuade people to do difficult things. We just need to teach them how to use that influence to change their lives and the lives of their fellow prisoners. We have assumed things about this fraternity that we knew nothing about, and we have judged them without knowing their story. I hate it when people do that to me.

I have friends behind the wire who are far better men than me. I know many who are more trustworthy, more righteous, and more honorable. I even have a friend who inspired me and truly changed before he was executed by the State of Alabama. Maybe we are going to see in our lifetime God fulfill the scripture that says, "God chose the foolish things of this world to shame the wise; God chose the weak things of this world to shame the strong. He chose the lowly things of this world and the despised things so that no one may boast before Him" (1 Corinthians 1:27–28, NIV). It's time to remove the stigma and shame from addiction, mental health, and incarceration.

Thousands of Beautiful Letters

The crown jewel of our POPP program is the graduation celebration after the men have worked hard to practice nonviolence for forty days at a time. Our shows are a thing to see. Imagine one hundred prisoners having a big party with brothers who were rivals only eight short weeks earlier. They have been working and preparing for this night, as this is their shining moment. Inmates are chosen to read their papers on their Champions of Peace, and it is quite an honor to be selected. Others will perform spoken word, skits, and special songs they have created. We bring in free-world food and they eat like kings: fried chicken, mashed potatoes, green beans, corn bread, and apple pie, with all the fixings. Many admit they began the program just for the food, but then they caught a vision. That doesn't bother me at all. Jesus used groceries too!

We also promise them we will have some special guests, or "dignitaries," to see their presentations. This is a huge deal for them, as many have never been recognized for their achievements or been rewarded for anything. Many admit this is the most significant thing they have ever accomplished. At the end of the celebration, the men receive what they have been working so hard for: the POPP Certificate of Achievement. This document has been given to probation and parole officers, potential employers, pastors, school admission boards, and more. Some of these hang on the walls of their cells, and obviously many have been sent home to their families, as this achievement makes them very proud. We know of several occasions where this certificate has helped graduates get approved for parole, and one was even downgraded to life with the possibility of parole, instead of life without that possibility. That brother now has hope again.

A significant part of our program is when the participants are required to write a paper on their Champion of Peace. They can choose one of the peacemakers we have studied throughout the project: Gandhi, King, Mandela, Mother Teresa, Dalai Lama, and others. Or they can choose a parent, grandparent, teacher from their childhood, or some other significant person who played a positive role in their life. Some have even chosen their warden. This is the magical part of our POPP graduation ceremony. They have the opportunity to show the world who they really are, and their brilliance is so powerful. When you see a hated, feared, and forgotten man, oftentimes a gang member, express what he believes and what he stands for, it is truly inspiring and something the free world needs to see. It is a powerful moment when they experience being admired and respected by their peers and special guests, many for the first time ever. They discover a new part of themselves that they might not have known existed: their noble self.

I have a box in my office where I have thousands of these papers written by inmates in prisons, jails, and detention centers across the nation. These letters reflect the changes these men have made and the convictions they have formed over the course of the project. These papers are some of my most valuable possessions, and they explain why I never judge an inmate by mere outward appearance. Many of the men chosen to participate were hard and protective at the beginning of the project, and many are covered with prison tats, even on their faces. You cannot see someone's insides until they show you—and you have to earn this right. Most times when we judge the cover, we get it totally wrong. This is one of my favorite parts of my calling: to uncover the beauty inside the most hardened men. It's a wonderful surprise as the present is unwrapped in front of my very eyes.

Most of all, I love to watch the faces of the dignitaries we invite to watch the graduation. What they expect to see is not what they see at all. At one of our recent graduations, a chief deputy sheriff got up in front of the men and said, "I'm going to be honest, when we first started this thing I didn't think some you could even read or write, much less complete the program." Then he got emotional. "Now, to hear the things you have written and to see the way you've expressed yourself, you have completely changed my view of you. I am so impressed, and I am so proud of you." This man has been working with inmates for over thirty years, and when given the chance to express themselves, these tough men brought him to tears with their words.

Once again, I was reminded that the world needs to see these men for who they truly are. The world needs stories of light in the darkness and hope in despair, and these stories have all that and more. Most have only seen how these men are portrayed in movies, on TV, or in rap videos, or games. Prison is as bad as you've seen and worse, but many of these men aren't. Behind the wire you'll find true heroes if you look hard enough, and those who have not figured out who they really are could be heroes too. They just need for someone to believe in them and be willing to give them a second chance—and don't we all want a second chance? People can change, even the ones who have done the most terrible things. They'll never be able to take back the things they've done or the wreckage they've caused, but maybe, just maybe, they can use the remainder of their lives to take care of their families and keep kids from making the same mistakes they made. There is always hope.

I also have a big box of Champions of Peace papers from over a thousand teens who have followed their lead. This is the proof in the pudding. These kids provide the motivation that sustains the movement behind the wire. I tell the brothers all throughout the project that they need a "big why" to continue pulling them to their dreams, and that they need to find purpose in their pain. The kids become that big why, and the purpose they lack. The brothers are desperate to make a difference, and when we call them to be role models, invariably they step up, or at least make an effort. Nobody has ever bothered to ask them to help.

I continue to remind them the kids are going through the same process they are, and that they have become their inspiration. I also remind the kids that the brothers behind the wire are literally putting their lives on the line for them, and not to let them down. You wouldn't believe how that charge inspires them.

I have hundreds of pictures of groups of joyful teens with peace signs in the air as they are set free from the stress and anxiety running rampant in their generation. I believe transformed criminals are an answer to teen violence on the streets, whether it be violence aimed at others or violence pointed at themselves. They need role models who have been there and done that, ones who speak their language and understand their pain.

Young POPP Peacemakers

Chapter Two
VIOLENCE IS NOT THE ANSWER

POPP was inspired by iconic peacemakers from around the world. When we first started, I was looking for a way to challenge the brothers by introducing them to others who have gone before them and fought this battle in the most intense environments, demonstrating that these principles actually work. They needed living, breathing examples to follow and proven methods to implement. That is what we provide for them. Every day they get quotes and action challenges from the greats like Dr. King, Gandhi, Mandela, the Dalai Lama, and other freedom fighters and world-changers. I didn't know at first if it would resonate with the brothers, but they devoured it. These men have nothing but time on their hands, and when challenged properly, they will use it to better themselves. I encourage them to do their daily homework in private if need be, in case they're worried about their gangster rep being damaged. The important thing is for them to put in the work, and then they'll reap what they sow. When you sow seeds of peace and hope, you will most definitely reap the harvest. It's a universal law.

A World Gone Mad

It's 2020, and it seems as if the whole world's gone mad. We reap what we sow, and we are reaping the whirlwind. Not since the turbulent sixties have we seen such violence and social unrest on our streets. I was a little boy when my hero and mentor Dr. Martin Luther King Jr. was assassinated in Memphis, Tennessee. I've been following his example since 1990, shortly after I graduated college. When they killed the Dreamer, it appeared as if his dream went silent for a while. The rage his death caused sparked a fire, and we've never seen his brilliant tactics effectively practiced on a large scale ever since, at least not like we witnessed then. He taught us that violence was not only un-Christlike, but it was impractical. We are seeing that played out on the big screen as we speak. He taught us that hate cannot drive out hate, only love can, and that darkness cannot drive out darkness, only light can. Right now the oppressed are using their rival's tactics. This only serves to embolden their oppressors and make them feel justified when they beat them down and lock them up.

Gandhi understood the power of peace when he nonviolently overcame his oppressors' tyranny. Mandela understood it when he modeled compassion and forgiveness to a nation on the brink of civil war, to people who were ready to exact revenge on their oppressors. Mandela had begun his campaign over thirty years earlier and was ready and willing to use violence to win his nation's freedom "by any means necessary," as brother Malcolm would say years later. But he, too, was transformed, and he shook hands with his former captor as they shared the Nobel Peace Prize in front of the whole world. It takes a master to pull that off.

Mandela followed one of his mentors, Mahatma Gandhi, as he had modeled for him years earlier: He made his enemies his friends. Dr. King emulated Gandhi as well as he dismantled Jim Crow in the racist South. King, Gandhi, and Mandela are inextricably bound by their unique styles of nonviolent resistance. They chose the difficult path, the same one Jesus chose over two thousand years ago. One giant learning from another.

In the Middle and Connected on All Sides

In the midst of the most volatile time our country has seen in decades, I am standing in an interesting position. More than ever before, labels are being carelessly thrown around in America. People are behaving as if one size fits all, and judging one another is at an all-time high. Pick a label and put it on: Republican or Democrat, red or blue, conservative or liberal; black, white, or brown; Christian, Muslim, or Jew; gay, straight, or other; legal or illegal; rich or poor; black lives, blue lives, or all lives; capitalist or socialist—the list goes on and on, with more labels popping up every day. It's as if you can sum a person up with a careless moniker and know everything about that person by the label you have identified them with. Nobody appreciates being labeled and defined, but we see more and more of it every day.

Here's the problem with that dangerous practice: There are many different kinds of Republicans and many types of Democrats; there are many types of Black Lives Matter adherents and many different kinds of officers; there are many types of Christians and many types of Muslims; and there are many, many different types of prisoners. When you label someone, you negate them. Can I really know everything there is to know about your character or your values based on your political affiliation? Can I judge your life or know what you hold dear based on your religious or gender orientation? I firmly believe we all have very good reasons for what we believe or where we stand on these critical issues. If I walk with you, and you let me in on your unique journey, then I will begin to understand why you believe what you believe. Many roads lead us to the place where we stand. I do not accept labels, and I will not be defined by how you see me.

My position is fairly unusual when it comes to these issues dividing our nation. I was raised on the right by a Republican family with conservative values. I spent fifteen years in the full-time ministry as a Christian Evangelist. I was born and raised in a red state, and everyone looked like me in the schools I attended. If you judged me by that résumé, you would get it all wrong. Over the years I have been embraced by the left because of my work with at-risk youth, prison reform, and my service to underserved communities. I have been the minority in the majority of my work, which has been one of the greatest blessings of my life.

I have strong ties and great relationships with police chiefs and sheriffs, but I also spoke at an NAACP Juneteenth Rally with Black Lives Matter. I work with pastors as well as gangsters. I serve with judges and other elected officials on both sides of the aisle. I also work with youth, and they have their own strong opinions about this current divide in America. Recently I have been challenged to pick a side, by both sides, but I refuse to do so. Who am I going to choose? I can't turn my back on law enforcement, because my work with them is important, and I am friends with many of them and worship with some. I won't turn my back on the NAACP or my brothers and sisters who happen to be liberal, as they have supported my work for so long. I will never leave my brothers behind the wire, as I have promised to support them for the rest of my days, and I will never leave the youth, who I am also forever committed to. I will never turn on my pastors, because we are family, and I will never forsake my Muslim brothers, who are a crucial part of my work and a powerful force in prisons across our land.

So, when I am challenged to choose a side, I will not. I will inhabit the middle and stand on my convictions, not labels. Some claim I lack conviction, and that's why I stay in the middle. To them I say look at my body of work, and you will see that I am prepared to die for what I believe in. I stay in the middle because from there I can have influence on all sides. I choose to discuss issues and individuals, not party lines. I refuse labels, because they cause division and are never truly representative of where an individual stands at any given time on any particular issue.

Gandhi, King, and Mandela

I cannot overstate the influence and power these three civil-rights icons have behind the wire. It's because, on some level, the brothers feel as though they can relate to their pain. When they see the way these three did time, even when their incarceration was intentional, it gives them a vision for how they can do their time. At least they know it's possible and that somebody has gone before them to show them the way.

Gandhi, King, and Mandela all used their time while imprisoned to arouse the world's conscience. They showed us how to suffer, and they modeled the power of nonviolent resistance. We talk about Dr. King's "Letter from a Birmingham Jail," and the brothers are inspired. They see how Mr. Gandhi was willing to die from starvation rather than live another day under colonial rule. They see the way Mr. Mandela was offered freedom three different times and still refused to leave prison until apartheid was no more. They see how Dr. King and his followers would intentionally get arrested—peacefully—to fuel their movement.

They also get a chance to learn about world-changing peacemakers such as Malcolm X, the Dalai Lama, Rabbi Heschel, Thich Nhat Hanh, Black Elk, Mother Teresa, Albert Einstein, Maya Angelou, Cesar Chavez, and others. Their imaginations are activated, and they are inspired and challenged when they see the power these men and women wielded while not resorting to violence. Some will say, "Malcolm and Mandela were violent along the way." True, but then we see their transformation into peacemakers, which makes them even more powerful in the brothers' eyes.

Mr. Gandhi taught us that when we suffer unjustly, and do it peacefully, it arouses something inside of spectators. He was moved by the example of Jesus and the power that selfless suffering has to overcome the hatred of our enemies. However, it seems no one wants to hear a message of peace these days. They've had enough, and I can't really blame them. The question is, will a strategy of violence bring about the desired result during these troubled times? Dr. King reasoned that while being immoral, violence is also impractical. The oppressor is always going to have more guns, more bodies, more money, more resources, and more time. Fighting against an enemy that has all the weapons is futile and ineffective. Even Sun Tzu taught that in his famous work *The Art of War*. Never fight a battle you cannot win. Instead, we employ means that confuse our enemies and win the masses to our cause. Suffering for a just cause carries tremendous power, while violence only emboldens and justifies the means of the oppressor.

I wish you could see the brothers come alive when they study these champions of peace. They learn to handle conflict in a different way, and before long the "spectators" (their rival inmates) are inspired by the courage it takes to make a peaceful stand. Please understand, they do not back down from an altercation. Instead, they learn to use their minds and words to diffuse and deescalate, and perhaps even win over their rivals. That gives them a brand-new kind of power, and onlookers want some of the same.

The Power of Nonviolent Reconciliation

These three peacemakers are heroes of mine, and they have become the pillars of the POPP program behind the wire: Gandhi for his groundbreaking philosophy of Satyagraha, or Soul Force; Dr. King for his monumental work in American civil rights and the landmark legislation he brought about; Mandela for his twenty-seven years of incarceration, which prepared him to tear down apartheid in South Africa and bring together a nation on the verge of civil war. These giants become much-needed role models for our prisoners who are fighting to change a dark and broken system of their own. Imagine how the brothers behind the wire feel when they are following and emulating these world-changers. They are inspired when they hear Mandela say, "In my country we go to prison first and then become president."

Violence Is Impractical and Futile

I am deeply concerned by the things we are seeing with frightening regularity in the media. The rioting, looting, and destruction of property by this young generation is garnering more and more attention, and many are beginning to believe this is the only way to truly change things in America. As I witness the useless violence erupting after dark on the streets of Portland, Seattle, New York City, and other American cities, it breaks my heart and worries me for the future.

This is the nature of violence. It emboldens the enemy while turning bystanders' attention away from the issues at hand and toward their justified anger. Peace, on the other hand, has the power to transform even the hardest heart. My life was changed when I learned of the courage of heroes like Medgar Evers, Rosa Parks, John Lewis, and so many others as they stood up to evil.

They ignited a flame in me that has never gone out and burns even brighter today. I fear we are losing their message as that beautiful generation passes away.

I believe many protesting on the streets today are cowards, and not heroes. It's so easy to pick up a brick, start a fire, or punch and kick a person who is down and defenseless. These are by no means the kinds of protests that yesterday's civil-rights leaders bled for, and even died for. Not even Malcolm X preached this kind of violent retaliation. I do not believe he would be looting, stealing, and destroying property to make his point if he were with us today. I believe his way would be deliberate, strategic, and methodical based on all the things he preached and modeled for us, even before he embraced nonviolence prior to his assassination.

Rage affects our ability to make rational decisions. When we give in to rage, our minds become clouded by emotion, and we can no longer see clearly to navigate through the storms. The solution always lies above the level of the problem, and Dr. King understood that. Violence begets more violence, and hatred only gives birth to more hate. The rage we are witnessing on the streets is not a carefully constructed plan of attack, but rather an emotional release of pent-up anger. While emotionally satisfying, anger and rage lack the ability to bring about true sustainable change, and that is why neither Gandhi, King, nor Mandela chose this mode of operation.

What impresses me so much about Mandela is the way he continued to change personally, eventually winning over his enemies with his methods. If he had gone right back to his militant ways after getting out of prison and sought revenge on those who had enslaved him, the nation would have erupted into a bloody civil war, as many desperately wanted. The likely result? Those who held power would have prevailed once again, and he would've been killed as a revolutionary. He might have been hailed as a martyr, but would have missed out on his true purpose to liberate the nation he so loved. As it was, he changed his approach, won the Nobel Peace Prize, was elected president, and went on to dismantle apartheid. His way prevailed, and he inspired the whole world through reconciliation rather than vengeance.

These violent agitators, not the BLM peaceful demonstrators, choose to come out at night, rather than in the light of day. Why is that? Because they can hide their evil deeds in the darkness. I admire nonviolent brothers and sisters, white, black, and brown, who march during the day and go home at night. After dark, these bad actors take away any power and influence that true Black Lives Matter protestors have gained during the day. Those who watch on TV conclude that the whole movement must be violent and dangerous, and everyone is discredited. History has proved time and time again that violence is not an effective means of overturning an unjust system.

Some say we need to let them lash out and "get it out of their system," and I understand that sometimes this might need to happen. However, we have seen over three months of nightly violent confrontations as I write these words. This is not blowing off steam or releasing pent-up anger, but rather an excuse to continue causing trouble with no clear agenda. To the agitators I would say, "Okay, you've gotten your nation's attention and you have thoroughly made your point. Now it's time to use this leverage to begin dialogue around your demands and potential solutions. Otherwise, you aren't really looking for change, you just want a reason to tear things up."

Solutions in South Africa

When I was in Durban, South Africa, for the 2012 Gandhi Global Peace Summit, I had a discussion that took my passion for the POPP movement to a whole new level. Dr. Bernard Lafayette, who was one of Dr. King's right-hand men and one of our hosts and organizers, told me that the last thing Dr. King said to him on the day he was assassinated was, "Bernard, the next thing we need to do is institutionalize nonviolence." And then he said to me, "Young man, don't stop doing what you're doing. We have yet to fulfill Martin's last wish. You are taking his dream into the prisons, and as far as I know, no one has ever done that. Please don't quit." Ela Gandhi, Mr. Gandhi's granddaughter, said roughly the same thing to me. I take that charge very seriously.

I was involved in a roleplay with Dr. Lafayette at that conference, and it was in front of an audience. He gave me a hypothetical scenario about a college where we were trying to bring about policy change for the students. He was illustrating the Kingian method for direct action campaigns.

Step one, he taught us, is information gathering. We can never mount a successful campaign until we have all the facts. We need to find out who the players are and what they are doing, or have done, to violate the rights of the students. We need to learn exactly what the issues are and determine potential solutions to the problem. We need to know how long it's been going on, and what has been done to try to change it to date.

In today's world, all it takes is a video, and people hit the streets without any real information. That is the lazy way, and you have no way to mobilize and control the demonstrators. With a video, you have no context. What happened before and after? What precipitated the event that was recorded? Was it a random act or something that happens regularly? Direct action with no facts or strategy is not only destined to fail, but it can cause more damage than the original infraction.

Just imagine what is going to happen when "deep fake" videos are released that look real, and young people have learned to hit the streets every time a new one is released. We are seeing in our country how violence erupts during poorly planned protests, especially when there are bad actors and fringe elements bent on destruction and chaos. When chaos begins, there is no way to separate the peaceful protesters from the rioters and looters. Dr. King organized nonviolent marches with extreme discipline among his demonstrators so as to accomplish their goals and bring about desired results. As it is today, there is no true leader and no real strategy, which dooms the campaign from the start.

Step two is negotiation. Once we have all the facts, then we can decide on appropriate demands and, more importantly, realistic ones. In one of the prisons, before we started POPP, the men decided to "sit down" and issue demands. They refused to go to their work details, and they went on strike. They stayed in their cells and food was brought to them. After about a week, the warden locked all the cells and decided to wait them out. Their campaign failed because their demands weren't realistic, they had no real strategy, and they had no established leaders. They wanted better meals, pay for their jobs, and conjugal visits. Men who crossed the picket line were beaten. There was no way they were ever going to get number three, so eventually they gave in and went back to work. (I am in no way encouraging prison protests, as I don't see any way to go up against such a formidable foe with no leverage. It is bound to fail. Instead, we must transform the system from the inside out, one man at a time.)

In the negotiation phase we must talk to the right parties who have the authority to bring about the desired result. Without realistic demands to the right people, there is no way to get what you want. In today's protests, these young people often have no real leadership, the line of communication with the right parties has not been established, and they're asking for things that those in charge don't even have the ability to deliver. These are lazy protests with no unified voice, and unrealistic demands that are destined to fail. We saw this illustrated when a city block of Downtown Portland was taken over by protestors and held as an autonomous zone. Eventually it failed because they hadn't come up with any realistic demands, and there was no unified voice. It was more of a mob mentality, something that evolved out of the chaos. Eventually someone was killed, and they were cleared out. This only weakened their movement and discredited their cause.

Step three is self-purification. If we have gathered all the facts, constructed a list of demands, and presented them to the appropriate parties, but all negotiation has failed, it is now time to prepare for direct action. This is the practice the demonstrators put in *before* they hit the streets. They had to be prepared to march nonviolently and endure brutal attacks so the nation would witness it and be appalled. This would give them powerful leverage, which would be invaluable to the struggle.

When they sat at those lunch counters, they had to be prepared not to retaliate with violence if the campaign was to succeed. When they boarded the buses for the freedom rides, they had to be prepared for whatever was waiting for them on the other end. When they marched into Birmingham where the hoses, rocks, dogs, and billy clubs would be used, they had to be prepared to carry out the strategy of nonviolent resistance. Today there are no such trainings, and there is no commitment to nonviolence. As it is, you have a mixed bag of peaceful demonstrators, along with looters, rioters, and criminals, and no real plan with no real leadership. How in the world is this young generation going to create sustainable change if they handle themselves recklessly with no leadership, no structure, no accountability, and no defined path to victory? Dr. King's method took more time, planning, and effort, but it was effective.

Step four is direct action. Once the first three steps have been completed, then we are ready for a successful campaign. In Montgomery, the change they were fighting for was to give people of color equal rights in the public transit system. In Memphis, they were fighting for equality for the sanitation workers who were being mistreated and drastically underpaid for their labor. Montgomery was a success, though it took over a year of boycotting the buses to finally break their opponents' will. In Memphis, on the other hand, the march turned violent and it was a disaster, which broke Martin's heart. After Dr. King was killed there, they finally got what they were asking for, but only after paying an incredibly heavy price.

If we shortcut the process and put step four first, we lose all credibility and influence with those who hold the power. Without all the facts, with no realistic demands delivered, and with no real plan to prepare the participants to bring about a peaceful demonstration, it becomes nothing more than an angry and disruptive rally that eventually dies out. You end up empowering the authorities to use whatever tactics they deem necessary to put down the protest, and no sustainable change will be realized. Violence is simply not practical as an effective strategy to change an unjust system.

Chapter Three
THE SEVEN POPP PRINCIPLES

The foundation of the POPP prison movement is the seven Power of Peace Principles. Step programs have proven effective, as evidenced by the twelve-step recovery movement. People in recovery value a process they can be accountable to and that measures their progress, so I borrowed that idea from Alcoholics Anonymous (AA). Deliberate step work and accountability have become the process for my different forty-day programs. I currently have three forty-day POPP projects: one for prisons, one for schools, and one for churches, all with different steps for each. In this chapter we will be looking at the seven steps that have proven effective in our prison program.

The Medicine for What's Killing Us

Things are quickly spiraling out of control in America. The country is heavily divided over several monumental issues. As I write this, we are in the middle of an election where it seems as if there is no positive outcome. Both sides are dug in, and no one is listening. At night we see the streets exploding with racial tension and rage against the police. Our nation is dealing with COVID-19, systemic racism, police brutality, a contentious election, and a potential economic collapse. Any one of these things would be enough to keep us up at night, but we are dealing with all of these at once. These are the most pressing and important issues many of us have ever faced. So, what is the solution? What is the medicine for what's killing us? We'll take a peek behind the wire for answers and potential solutions—a place where few, if any, have thought to look.

In my first prison in Georgia, we faced a real crisis. The gang violence had gotten so bad at one point that they locked the whole prison down for over a year. The inmates had no visitation, recreation, chow hall, church services, or any other gathering during that time, meaning effectively all 1,200 men were in solitary confinement with their cellmates. The violence got out of hand as the Gangster Disciples and Muslims were at war, and an inmate was killed during the month of Ramadan. That sparked off four more retaliatory killings over the next month. Already the number-one gang prison in the state, this institution became one of the bloodiest prisons in the country. This is the prison where we would develop the principles that would work in other prisons around the nation.

To say this setting was a challenge would be an understatement. However, I had the benefit of not knowing what I didn't know, so I had no idea it would be practically impossible to bring peace to this place. That naïveté turned out to be a good thing, because I might not have even tried had I known the probability of success. So, I developed my seven Power of Peace Principles with these brothers in the toughest prison in the state, and miraculously, they worked. We were on to something, and it was something brand new in the prison system at large. By the end of that year this prison won Institution of the Year, literally going from worst to first.

I've faced considerable opposition over the years, and these principles are what protected me. I have made it very hard for these men to hate me, as I pose no threat. I dare them to test the principles and promise them that if they adopt these steps as a way of life, everything in their world will improve. These steps and the process that follows were born out of experience, trial and error, and experimentation. There was no model for us to follow; we were making it up as we went along, testing, approving, and revising.

Our laboratory was the small chapel on Friday mornings with the most powerful and influential men in the prison. There were never any officers present, because the warden trusted the leaders in our group. There were threats everywhere, all the time, to inmates as well as staff. The fact that there were no keys in the room turned out to be a big deal. The men won't express themselves openly and honestly if the police are present. The warden let us try unconventional methods, and I am forever grateful to him for that. Those moves, and other bold ones he made during his tenure, ended up getting his prison an award and himself a promotion.

Practicing These Principles in All My Affairs

I have been forced to practice these conflict resolution techniques as a way of life, because if I didn't, the consequences could have been dire. These are not principles I read in a book or things I was taught in school. Rather, these are tried, tested, and true core beliefs I have lived out in some of the most intense, and potentially dangerous, environments with people who have the means, motive, and ability to cause me harm. This has made all the difference. I have practiced these principles with death-row inmates and cartel soldiers, with gang leaders and hitmen, with killers and kidnappers, with terrorists and psychopaths. My teachings come from experience in the most real situations with the most real men, and that is why this process has become a natural way of life for me, though it is still hard to practice at times.

Now, with recent current events, these Power of Peace Principles have become much more relevant. My conflict-resolution strategies are now in demand in the free world, as we all have been beaten into a state of reasonableness and are open to new ideas. I am now being engaged to teach my POPP Principles to pastors and coaches, CEOs and police officers, parents and their kids, local government, and even the Environmental Protection Agency. Conflict is part of life and always has been, but nowadays it seems as if the stakes are higher. One misstep can be disastrous.

The POPP Peace Council

The POPP Prison Peace Council consisted of fifteen men, and we had permission from the Department of Corrections to invite the men we chose. The warden and deputy warden of security helped us choose the men based on their influence. Our partnership with administration was crucial so that they could encourage the men when they saw them trying to change, especially those who were causing the most trouble. When we began changing the minds of the gang leaders, we quickly began to change the minds of those who followed them. In our first thirty days, there were no stabbings. This prison hadn't gone so long without a stabbing for as long as anyone could remember. Now we had the warden's attention and support, and the movement continued to progress. I cannot overstate how important it is to have the full support of the warden and their staff. We'll never bring about sustainable change if we can't work together effectively with the powers-that-be. Dr. King knew that, as he worked with governors, pastors, and eventually the president to bring about historic civil-rights legislation.

In the summertime in Georgia the prisons get very hot. Most of the dorms don't have air conditioning, so it is not uncommon to have one-hundred-degree heat in the cells. Imagine trying to sleep under those conditions on a thin, hard mat and a rubber pillow. So, naturally, violence spikes as the temperature rises; the men are uncomfortable, on edge, and angry. On top of that, in the year we started the movement, the state had recently outlawed tobacco in the prisons, so the brothers were unusually agitated. Add to that whenever a gang war started in one prison in the state, it would spread to others, and it always popped off at this prison, especially in the heat. With all that against us, the magic happened.

During the summer of 2011 it got so peaceful inside this violent prison that the captains actually thought their walkie-talkies weren't working. It turns out they were working just fine; there just wasn't anything to report. The brothers laid it down and started to realize life was better when they weren't beefing. The POPP Peace Council put down potential wars, called off attacks, and resolved disputes nonviolently before they became physical, and often before the authorities even knew they were brewing. Imagine how valuable that is to a warden.

The only way we're going to see true prison reform in our nation is to get prison officials *and* prisoners to work together, and I've seen it work beautifully. However, both sides must demonstrate that they truly want reform. Here is a process I have seen work time and time again, but only when administration supports it. I use the words "rival," "adversary," "opponent," and "enemy" because we are working with rival gangs in maximum-security prisons.

1) *Seek First to Understand Your Opponent*

The first step in the process is to gather information about my opponent, so I can come from a position of understanding. This is essential if I want to influence my rival and win them over to my position, or if they are going to have an opportunity to change my mind. If I study the other, trying to learn as much about them as possible, then I will move into a position of power when we discuss issues and potential solutions. Regardless of whether the other intends to cooperate, negotiate, or even talk again, it is still wise to seek first to understand them. If this isn't the right time for action or reconciliation, then at least I will be better prepared when the opportunity arises. The better I understand my opponent, the easier it will be to present my case when the time comes.

In order to understand the other's journey, I will need to ask good questions and pay attention to everything they're willing to offer me. I make it my goal to become an expert on their position. I already know what I believe, what I think, and how I feel. I have no idea what the other believes, thinks, or feels, so it is wise for me to hold my tongue and ask good questions. Too many times I have gone into a confrontation where all I was focused on was my position and my desired outcome. Knowing little about my opponent puts me in a weaker position because I have no idea what is important to them: their objectives, their pain points, their desired outcomes, or their ideas for solutions. My objective is not to win the exchange, but rather to get familiar with who they are, and what they want, and why, if at all possible.

In order to accomplish this power move, it must be authentic. This technique will backfire if it is not genuine. Therefore, I must truly care about the other's journey, which takes a certain amount of humility. This is about turning my enemy into my friend, so if the objective is to win them over, then it makes sense that I go

The New Convict Code

ahead and start treating them as a friend. I am genuinely interested in the human adventure, and I have lots of experience making friends with the toughest cases. My process always begins with this step, and it is one of my favorite parts of our prison program. I love making friends with the hard to reach; the tougher, the better. I consider it a challenge, and a game. *Try not to be my friend. I dare you.*

I have made it my practice to treat those who get the least respect with special honor, going out of my way to treat them respectfully. They don't have to earn it; I freely give it. I've had success working with those who are tough to work with simply because I showed special interest and gave them my undivided attention from the first moment. One of my favorite times is when I meet the men for the first time in a new prison. These are men chosen by the warden because they have power and influence. Imagine about a hundred men—black, white, and brown; Christian, Muslim, and Jew; Crips, Bloods, Latin Kings, Gangster Disciples, Aryan Brotherhood, and Nation of Islam, as well as other rivals from various other sets. It looks like something you would see in a movie, but even more fascinating.

They don't know why they've been chosen, but they have agreed to come to one two-hour event. Then they will choose whether they want to commit to the eight-week project. I begin to make my rounds and look each man in the eye, shake his hand, bow slightly, and call him "sir." My goal is to make every one of them laugh; that's the fun part. The tougher the man, the more of a challenge, and I use humor to disarm the dangerous. This way, as soon as I address the group, I know I have made a personal connection with every guy in the room. Hate and judgment happen at a distance; respect and honor happen up close and personal.

What would happen if I treated these men like they were

dangerous and unpredictable? They would know it and live down to my expectations. But if I treat them with special honor and respect, then they behave accordingly. I believe we all do that.

The Young Muslim Imam

One of the most crucial parts of the process when I'm launching a peace initiative in a new prison is to identify the most influential prisoners and get them into the program. Once I get the right brothers in the room, then it's time to engage them and begin winning their respect. Without the leader's respect, our chances of creating sustainable change are low or nonexistent.

At one particular launch it was very important for me to win the support of the Muslim brothers, because they carry lots of weight in this particular state. I asked a trusted brother who the imam was, and he pointed him out and also vouched for him as an intelligent and reasonable brother. So, I asked for an introduction and began to chat him up. He was about thirty (rare for a prison imam), articulate, and happened to be black. He was easy to talk to and it was easy to make him laugh, which for me is an important part of the process. As it has been said, "People will not long remember what you did or what you said, but they will remember forever how you made them feel." So, laughter and joy are a wonderful place to begin when forming a working relationship with a new friend.

I wasted no time and asked the imam for a favor. You'd be amazed how quickly people will help if you simply ask. He asked what he could do for me, and I said, "I want to learn more about Islam. Would you be willing to teach me things I may not know? We can chat each time I come to the prison, if you'd like. I would greatly appreciate that." It was a sincere request, and it had an immediate impact. This man was almost half my age, a brother of more color, a prisoner, and had a different faith tradition than my own. I was defining the nature of our relationship from the start, and he saw it would be based on humility, respect, and admiration. He immediately agreed, and I said, "Can we start right now?"

He smiled and said, "Absolutely." He went on to explain the way Muslims see Jesus, and how they hold him in such high regard. He said, "Most Christians think we don't believe in Him, which is completely false. We believe Jesus will return one day, just as you do, and take the chosen to paradise. We believe Muhammad is the *last* prophet, but not greater than Jesus. We revere Him."

I told my new friend I could not presume to know things I have never learned and that he would be a valuable asset and advisor to me if he was willing. He was more than willing, and I count him as my friend to this day. Seek first to understand your opponent. It will lead you into a position of power and influence.

2) *Find Common Ground with Your Adversary*

The second step in the reconciliation process is to find common ground with the other. In today's political climate, I see very little of this. Instead, people have programmed their brains to look for differences rather than similarities, and we always find what we look for. If I look for the things with your stance that I disagree with, and begin to oppose those things, then I lose any influence I might have had to win you over. Just like understanding my opponent's viewpoint as well or better than they do puts me in a position of power, the same is true if I find issues we agree on first and make note of those. It even strengthens your standing if you point these similarities out and illustrate the points on which you agree.

I love asking interesting questions when seeking to disarm a potential rival. In a prison setting, an easy topic is sports. I'll find out where they are from and begin asking about the teams they pull for. After that, it's easy to get them laughing when I tell them who my teams are and then bring up common opponents or funny stories about their team. This isn't difficult, and it lightens the mood when preparing for a tough conversation. I love inquiring about where they are from and where their family line originated. This makes for interesting conversation to either learn about a place I do not know, which puts them in an expert position, or relate to them about a place I have been to. People love to talk about themselves, and you'd be surprised how people will share things about their lives if you only ask specific questions, especially with difficult relationships. The one who talks the most in a conversation typically walks away feeling the best about that exchange. It's never weak to show interest in another's journey, especially when interacting with a potential rival.

An effective illustration I use in prisons is the following. I'm in front of a hundred men all wearing white with a blue stripe, many of whom are rivals from different organizations on the chain gang. I begin by saying they all bleed red, live in the same place, and wear the same clothes. Most if not all of them have strong negative feelings and opposition toward the correctional officers, all of them want to go home as soon as possible, and all of them have family they care about on some level. So, we start there. And then I paint a picture of all of us being put on a plane and flown into a hostile environment (typically I choose North Korea because of that country's stance on outsiders). Then I say, "If they dropped us all off in the middle of that country and flew away, what would we do?"

It is unlikely that we would divide ourselves up by race, religion, age, or gang affiliation. Most likely we would stick together, come up with a plan, and even choose leaders to follow. The whole game would be survival and self-preservation. Fighting, arguing, conflicts, and beefs would be tabled until we got out of danger.

The obvious conclusion comes next: You live in a hostile environment with considerable threats, so what if we focus on what we have in common and take care of the most obvious threats, and then we can deal with the smaller issues? It makes sense to them; they've just never considered that strategy is even possible. It most certainly is. Find common ground with your adversary; two are better than one.

Chava's Field

The Party on Chava's Field

Tijuana has been such a valuable and important part of my work. I began going across the border between San Diego and Tijuana in 2016. My friend Jeff Wadstrom had been working that field for several years, and knew many of the players and the lay of the land. The cartels already knew who he was and why he was there, and did not see him as a threat. Our partner and friend there has ties to the cartel that controls the city because people from his past are still connected to that life. He has their respect and trust, and he has vouched for us, which keeps us safe.

The area where my friends do most of their work is called Terrazas, and anyone who knows Tijuana will tell you it doesn't get any rougher than that particular area. It has become a cartel battleground, and the kids who live there are caught in the crossfire. The families there are very poor, and the children are at great risk of being kidnapped and trafficked, or recruited as soldiers for the cartels. The kids we work with are part of a soccer club called Letics, and one of the fields they use is right in the middle of that hot spot. A little store located by that field is a meeting place where the rival cartels have met to converse face to face. I was once hidden in that store when the federales were rounding up people to extort, and being Americans, we were natural targets. Down there it's often hard to tell the good guys from the bad guys.

We wanted to do something to win the trust and respect of that little community, so we planned to have a big party with games, sports, music, and food for the children. However, there was one major obstacle in our way: If we didn't get the blessing of the cartel soldier who controls that area, then we would definitely be in danger. That would be a sign of disrespect, and we could not afford that. So, we got the word out that we needed to meet with whoever was in charge. The man who controlled that area had recently fled, as there was a price on his head. He was recently executed. We had to find out who had replaced him. The answer was a young man named "Chava." He was known to be potentially dangerous. We got word to him and asked for a meeting.

The day came, and we headed for the field. It is open and

The New Convict Code

visible, surrounded by walls tagged with graffiti and burnt-out buildings. There are always beautiful children playing, but not many adults milling around. The field is all dirt with no grass for the players. It felt like we were in a movie, perhaps an old Clint Eastwood film! Finally, we spotted Chava, and he made his way across the field toward us. My friend Jeff and I made our way toward him, along with Jesus, our interpreter. As we met, I extended my hand, and hesitantly, he shook it. He did not know why he was there or what we wanted from him; he had just been told we wanted a meeting.

I began by telling him we knew who he was and that he ran things around there. I told him I respected him and would not dare make a move in his neighborhood without his blessing. I told him of our intentions and that we wanted to do something special for his people, especially the children. We told him we would like to do this as a gesture of respect, and that this gift to the children would be in his honor, as if he were feeding them himself. I was putting him in a position of respect and giving him the power in this interaction, just like I had learned in the prisons.

As he listened through our interpreter, he got distracted by my tattoo sleeve. He was focused on one particular part of it that had the word "paz," which means peace in Spanish. He nodded as if to ask, *Why do you have that?*

I replied, "Because I come in peace. It is for you." He nodded his head approvingly. I looked at his forearm and saw the word "Lupita." I nodded as if to say, *And why do you have that?* He looked over at a wall and the young lady sitting against it. I said, "Is that Lupita?" He nodded, and I smiled. I asked, "Is she your girlfriend?"

He said, "We're getting married." Now we were connected, and he was letting me into his life, if only a little bit.

I went on to tell him about my tattoo and how it is a tribute to everyone who has helped to build the Power of Peace movement. I told him we had brothers inside of La Mesa prison there in Tijuana, as we had worked with the men in there. I showed him the tattoo on the back of my arm I had put there for the men of La Mesa. This brought immediate respect from him.

Then I took a chance. "If you allow us to use your field, and let us do this for your people, then I will do something for you. When I return next month, I will have a special gift for you. I will have a tattoo right here, in your honor, and it will say 'Lupita.'" There was an uncomfortable pause, and then he began to smile, and then he broke into laughter. I was so glad he got the joke! We gave each other the gangster hug, and now I had a friend. The next day we filled the field with children, music, laughter, and tacos. And he sat beside that same wall and watched it all. We tried to get him to come over, but he would not. So, we took him a plate of tacos and offered it to him. He declined, but thanked us for the offer.

We had treated him respectfully, and he had shown us the same. I went back to see him the next month and they said he was gone, arrested for murder and sent to La Mesa. It turned out he didn't do the murder, though he was present. I recently got word that he's out. I sent a message back to him that I wanted to see him again. We had found common ground and worked from there.

Prison Tats and the Secret of My Sleeve

The POPP Tattoo: The Power of Peace

Tattoo artists are in high demand in the prison system, and tattoo art is a good hustle if you have skills. A tattoo gun can be made out of a pen, a paper clip, and a CD player motor, along with burnt baby oil for the ink. Some of the artists are really talented, and prison tats often have significance. In Russian prisons, the tattoos typically represent the charge you were convicted of. A tattoo of Mother Mary can mean you were convicted of murder, for example. When I was in Ukraine, I quickly learned that those with tattoos had most likely done time, so I got strange looks everywhere I went! Authorities take pictures of inmate tattoos when they are processed through intake, as they look for gang signs and affiliations.

When the prison peace movement began to take off at our first prison, I got a tattoo on my wrist as a tribute to the first POPP prisoners. It is a broken peace sign with a "40" in the middle to signify our "Forty Days of Peace" program, which had become our flagship. I believed it would be the only one, and I even told my wife that. As the movement spread to three prisons in Michigan, I felt compelled to do the same for their contribution, and I got "Mighty Men of Muskegon" right above the first one. But as we made our way to juvenile prisons in Ohio, I did the same thing. It became an important part of the program, and an inspiration to the brothers. I would commit to them, "If you give your best effort to live nonviolently for forty days, and to help others do the same, then when I come back to see you, I'll have you on my arm forever." They were amazed.

Now, all these years later, I have a full sleeve up to my shoulder and all the way around my arm, down to my wrist. I have prisons, schools, rehab facilities, famous peacemakers, other countries, faiths, cultures, symbols, our logos, books I have written, and more. It has become a living, breathing tribute to hated, feared, and forgotten brothers of mine behind the wire. It proves to them that I will never forget them or forsake them. We've even had inmates cover up their gang tattoos that do not represent them anymore, and some have gotten new peace tattoos of their own. It has become my signature and my trademark, and my special gift to this misfit band of brothers across the nation who saved my life. I even have one for the brothers in the cartel prison in Tijuana, and it is one of the most special ones I wear.

I tell people that if they look closely, they will find themselves in my tattoo. It has connected me with a death row inmate who was Muslim and saw the Arabic word "salam," which means peace. It has connected me with brothers in Ukraine as they see their symbol for peace. It has connected me with a South African brother who happened to be Zulu but saw the word "amani," which means peace in Swahili. There are so many more examples, but I do not have the time to tell them all. When I say, "I come in peace," you can believe me because it's written all over my arm. We have so much more in common than what separates us; I just wish people would come to believe that.

3) Walk a Mile in Your Enemy's Shoes before You Judge Him

We live in a day and age filled with profiling on both sides, and snap judgments based on nothing more than the color of your skin, color of your clothes (law enforcement), political affiliation, even whether you choose to wear a mask during the COVID-19 outbreak. In our prison programs, inmates are learning to suspend judgment until they know more about a man's journey. Judgment, hatred, and bias happen at a distance, but the closer you get to the other, the more you begin to understand them and possibly even relate to their journey and find compassion. I have developed a fascination for the other's journey and their unique story. The more different we are, the more fascinated I am. Albert Einstein said his greatest gift was that he was "passionately curious." I share that with him. Whether it be working with prisoners, or with young people in tough schools, I am fascinated to walk with them, listen, and learn.

The problem today is that everyone is shouting, and nobody is listening. It's lazy and cowardly, in my opinion, to sit back and criticize the other from behind the safety of your computer. Anyone can attack, but can you walk with the other in fascination and learn from a journey different from your own? This has been one of the greatest blessings of my life, to be able to grow close to people of so many backgrounds. What a sad life to only walk with those who look like you, believe like you, and vote like you. Many years ago, I set out to explore things I did not know. That led me on a journey around the world to study different cultures, faiths, and lifestyles. I have been in synagogues, mosques, cathedrals, temples, ashrams, and even a sweat lodge. I've learned from rabbis, imams, priests, monks, and shamans. How can I presume to know if I do not go? How can I judge the other when I know absolutely nothing about their unique journey? So, I set out to learn, understand, and become a student of the other, and that has made all the difference.

Anyone can practice this method; all it takes is humility. Why do people feel the need to defend, protect, and fight for their position against those who don't see things the same way? I know what I believe, I know what I think, and I know where I stand. However, I never want to stop learning and growing, and letting another teach me is no threat, and definitely not a weakness. There is no worst-case scenario. When a man feels respected, he has a hard time hating you. So, I walk with them and talk with them, and save judgment for later. That way, if I have been down the road with them, I'll be in a better position to make a correct judgment. Here is an example of men learning more about their rivals.

Stand or Kneel

Right around the time when Colin Kaepernick chose to kneel during the national anthem as a protest to police brutality and racism, I was part of an inspiring experiment inside Georgia's most dangerous maximum-security prison. Standing in front of sixty-four men wearing white with a blue stripe, I asked a question: "Please raise your hand if you refuse to stand during our national anthem." We chose six of the brothers who raised their hands and called them up front. Then I asked the brothers to raise their hands if they refused to kneel during the playing of that song. They came up front as well, and I asked them to choose a representative from

The New Convict Code

each side. We would have a debate, and the rest of the men would be the judges.

The rules were simple: Each speaker would get three minutes to make his point, and then each would get a one-minute rebuttal. There would be no interrupting, no slander or profanity, no gang references, and no words directed at any one individual. Each team got together for ten minutes and helped their speaker prepare his remarks, while the rest of us had a general conversation about the issue so everyone would be fully aware. The group was pretty much split right down the middle, with half choosing to kneel and half choosing to stand. We chose the order of speakers, and the debate was set.

The first to go chose to speak on the side of those who stand. He shared passionately about his time in the military as a medic and how he had dragged his buddies off the battlefield, some of them dying in his arms. He talked about his service to his country and his patriotism. He spoke of his family, and how he would never dishonor the memory of his comrades by kneeling in front of Old Glory. He made a compelling case, and all the men applauded him as he stepped away from the podium. This brother happened to be white. The second speaker came from a completely different angle, but had just as much conviction. He shared about how his little brother had been killed by a police officer while unarmed. Close to tears, but not crying, he spoke of his anger and loss, and said he would never stand for that song because he wanted everyone to see that flag in a new light. He said that until every American had the same rights and freedoms, he would kneel and try to get people to see his little brother. Once again, all the brothers applauded. He happened to be black.

Afterward I posed the same two options as I did when we

began: "Raise your hand if you would kneel, and raise your hand if you would stand."

Incredibly, about a third of the room had changed their minds. And then a hand went up and a brother said, "We never knew you were in the war, brother."

To which he replied, "You never asked."

In a short period of time, these prisoners had come together on an issue that is dividing the free world. Are you open and willing to change your mind if given a good enough reason? These men are. And by the way, they didn't break any of the debate rules. There were no interruptions, no ridicule or slander, no profanity, and absolutely no disrespect. We don't even see those rules obeyed in our presidential debates. As a beautiful gesture of their newfound unity, the one brother stood with his white hand over his heart, while his other hand rested on his brother's black shoulder as he knelt. It was an amazing thing to behold.

How are they able to come together behind the wire when we find it impossible to come together out here in the free world? Perhaps they're more grateful for the little things we take for granted every day. They were given a voice; maybe we don't bother to use ours constructively. They were given a choice; maybe we get so many of those every day that we don't even value them. We have much to learn from this band of brothers. Walk a mile with your enemy before you judge him. You might be surprised at what you learn.

4) *Practice Active Listening and Pause before Responding*

Active listening is becoming a lost art in today's culture. Listening means "I hear what you're saying," but active listening means "I am fully involved, engaged, and I'm receiving what you are communicating." This involves posture, eye contact, body language, nonverbal cues, and words of affirmation. When I know someone is truly listening to me, it helps me to better articulate my point while also preparing me to be more open to their response. In these troubling times it seems as if everyone has an opinion, but many are digging into their position and are prepared to fight to the death without even listening to their opponents. Facebook started out as a platform to connect with old friends and family, share pictures and memories, and rekindle old relationships. Now, for many, it has become a platform for fighting, criticizing, and even ridiculing. We teach our kids not to do that, but who do you think they're learning it from?

With all that is going on in our country, people have strong feelings regarding important issues, and most likely deep convictions as well. The stakes are higher than they've ever been in my lifetime, but is anyone actually listening? I decided somewhere along the way that I am open to changing my mind on any given issue, as long as you give me a good enough reason. Isn't that what we want from the other? We want to be heard, and we want others to truly listen to our opinion and join our side. However, the one on the other side of your argument feels exactly the same way and expects nothing less. It's not only right to listen, but it is wise.

Why wouldn't you want to know the other's position thoroughly before you persuade them? I teach the brothers that this is an important strategy. I poll them about everything I wish to learn about life behind the wire, because there's no way I can ever understand their world if I don't allow them to teach me. And they are eager to teach. However, if I don't listen, then I don't learn. I am trying to persuade them to do difficult things. Imagine how it would go for me if I did all the talking about their world without even understanding it. They surely wouldn't respect me and would most likely oppose me, concluding that I was a fraud. They have told me they're much more concerned about the brother watching quietly than the brother who runs his mouth all the time. The one who holds his tongue and pays attention is seen as more powerful than the big mouth who does all the talking. That can be hard for someone who talks for a living, but I must practice what I preach.

Have you ever found yourself in an emotionally charged conversation where it escalates, and you're just waiting for the other to take a breath so you can interrupt and interject with more volume? This tends to happen frequently with spouses; at least, it does with mine from time to time. This causes problems in relationships and leads to a communication breakdown, and sometimes an eventual breakup. What we need now more than ever—whether it's with law enforcement and Black Lives Matter, or with Congress up on the Hill, or between spouses in a troubled marriage—is good questions coupled with focused listening from both sides. Then asking more questions with even more active listening until we come to an understanding, at least regarding why the other feels so passionately about their position. No one is all right and no one is all wrong; the solution is typically somewhere in the middle. Otherwise, we become angry experts on what's wrong with the other and nothing more than critical complainers who have no real power to change anything.

My Mistake with the Crips

The peace initiative was rolling, and we were making progress well into our "Forty Days to Freedom" campaign at a maximum-security prison in the Southeast. Then there was a serious stall in the momentum. The brothers became complacent and stopped

The New Convict Code

putting in the work. So that Tuesday, when I made my way to the prison, I decided to be strong with my message and really challenge them in order to get their attention. Usually they not only allow me to bring it strong, but they respect it, and they like it that way. But this time was different. I hadn't been listening to the chatter or getting my intel like I normally would. I should have felt the vibe in the room and trusted my instinct, but I hadn't put in my work, either. I was on autopilot, which can be dangerous in a prison.

What I didn't know was that a group of about six Crips had been transferred into the dorm we were operating in. I didn't see them, and I didn't notice their energy or their expressions. That day I drew upon a football theme because we were right in the middle of the NFL playoffs and my Atlanta Falcons were trying to advance. I said, "We happen to have the same number of guys in this project as the Falcons currently have on their roster. I have to say, if we were a football team, and if we took an honest assessment of where we stand, I would say our team sucks right now. Now let's get off our butts and put in some real work!" I said it with passion and conviction. I went on to say, "If every man doesn't get engaged and put forth their best effort, then we're gonna get our butts handed to us!" Most of the guys were motivated and inspired and showed their enthusiasm, but a small group of guys didn't, and I still didn't see them. These Crips didn't know me, didn't know my style, and I hadn't won their respect yet nor earned the right to call them out like that. They didn't appreciate it.

The next week when I showed up, a few of my POPP leaders met me at the gate leading to their dorm. I trusted these brothers with my life. They said, "Bro, you don't need to go in there today. The Crips have rounded up about a dozen guys, and they have all turned in their wristbands." That had never happened before. These men love their POPP wristbands. They wear them with pride and protect them, as they typically aren't allowed to wear wristbands in maximum-security prisons. They are like a badge of courage for these brothers and highly valued. So, the fact that 20 percent of the participants had turned them in was significant. They continued, "If you go back there today, there could be a problem."

So, we went to the small room where we have our Peace Council meetings and had a really good talk. They assured me they didn't see it like the Crips did, and that they knew me and trusted my heart. They told me I had been a little too strong, and that the Crips took it as disrespect. They said there was a bit of a mutiny going on, and I needed to be more careful and watch my back. I asked them to deliver a message for me: "Please tell the Crips I am sincerely sorry I disrespected them. Tell them I would love a second chance to show them who I am. Communicate to them that I will learn from my mistakes, and they will see my repentance by my deeds." They thanked me for my humility and committed that they would pass along the message. I looked forward to the next meeting to make things right. I never got the chance.

I learned a valuable lesson: Do not take these men for granted, and respect the space in which I operate in. I had gotten too comfortable in a place where you should never be too comfortable. I did not change my energy, style, or conviction going forward, but I did recommit to being perceptive and shrewd in the way I deal with these potentially dangerous brothers. They had helped me become better at my craft, and so I am grateful for their stand. Failure is a valuable teacher.

Active listening is much more than hearing the words. It's

about nonverbal cues, body language, facial expressions, silence, and much more. If I had really been paying attention, and paused to consider my words, then things could have gone much differently. Live and learn.

5) *Practice Deliberate Communication and Use Your Influence for Peace*

Once I have sought first to understand, found some common ground, walked a mile with the other, and paid careful attention to what they have shared, now it is my turn to speak. When I do, I must use deliberate and intentional language to give them the best possible chance of receiving what I say. Hopefully at this stage of the conversation I have created an atmosphere of respect. Why in the world would I now use my precious words to ridicule, belittle, disrespect, or devalue my opponent? If the end goal is to come to some sort of resolution, and hopefully to win my rival over, then I should choose my words and tone carefully so as to pull my opponent closer. That way I will be in a much better position to persuade them to my position or change my position to theirs.

Dr. King was a master at this art. I cannot remember a time when he lost his cool or his temper, or gave way to his emotions. That is amazing to me, considering the fact that he faced daily death threats, lies, and plots, and was called disgusting names regularly. He was despised and constantly baited by his enemies, yet they never won. Even at the very end of his life, when he knew his time was short, he showed nothing but love and resolve while never losing his deep conviction, and hatred did not make him bitter. I long to be that strong and self-controlled.

We live in a world where people are looking for things to be offended by. It can be a tweet, a post, or a comment, and then spectators pounce, spewing vitriol and venom as if they have the right to behave that way. Not only is it wrong, but it is so ineffective. If I lose my temper, or get emotional and say things I shouldn't, then I drive my rival further into their position, and I lose ground. However, if I keep my cool while my opponent loses theirs, and I speak respectfully while not backing down from my position, I will shame my enemy, and our spectators will see things for what they really are. I might not win over my rival, but I might win over my witnesses. Either way, my opponent will have a harder time hating me, and I might put myself in a position for them to actually hear what I am saying.

Words are powerful and creative, and they carry vast potential. My words can build up or tear down; they can bring together or divide; they can encourage or deflate; they can diffuse or escalate; they can compliment or criticize; they can extinguish or enflame. I have the power to change a situation merely by the words and the tone I use. Nations have gone to war over careless words exchanged in a pivotal time of crisis. Proverbs 18:21 (NIV) says, "The tongue has the power of life and death, and those who love it will eat its fruit." How many relationships have been irreparably damaged by a few careless words offered in a heated exchange?

In POPP, the prisoners learn to use deliberate and intentional language when dealing with rivals in a confrontation. They admire the peacemakers we study, and they recognize that they were strong men. They learn that they can have even more power if they learn to tame the tongue and use their influence for peace. By practicing this one step, many altercations have been resolved, violence has been deescalated, and enemies have become friends. If inmates can practice this principle behind the wire, we can master it in the free world. They are becoming unlikely role models, and the key is humility.

Andre and the Situation

The Peace Council was running smoothly and violence was decreasing in a very dangerous prison. We would meet on Friday mornings weekly with some of the most powerful brothers representing the most powerful gangs. We would go around the table and discuss specific issues that had occurred, and try to find solutions before retaliations took place. I was amazed as orders were overturned by the shot callers, and peaceful solutions changed the tide from what had been a bloody year. Their influence led to a new peace that was gathering momentum.

A significant issue was raised at one of our meetings. Intel is vital to these inmates, and they have a sophisticated communication system so as to stay off the radar of administration and staff. They use a "kite" system—tiny, almost unreadable messages on tiny strips of paper that get delivered around the prison by brothers who have details that give them access to all the different parts of the compound. A kite had relayed to a certain dorm that they should be prepared, because a shakedown was coming in the middle of the night. I only learned of this after it happened, as I don't have access to inmate intel. When the Correctional Emergency Response Team (CERT) shakes down a dorm, they toss all the cells, looking for contraband: cell phones, drugs, weapons, cash, and other prohibited items. They come in the middle of the night, wake up the inmates, and line them up outside their cells while all their belongings get thrown around and oftentimes broken in the process. The brothers are left to put their cells back together, and those who have violations are sent to the hole. I have seen boxes filled with shanks, knives, and even a machete or two from these shakedowns.

So, here was the issue: Before the shakedown came that night, $3,000 cash was sent from that dorm to the neighboring dorm to protect it, which is typical. However, the next day the cash was not returned to its owner. This was a significant problem. Threats were made and ultimatums were issued, and things were about to get violent. Potentially, over fifty inmates could go to war with another fifty right next door. The brothers discussed it, and Andre, one of the leaders, stepped up and said he would handle it. The administration wasn't aware of the issue, and the gang leaders were doing what the officers would not have been able to handle. All security could have done was shake down the other dorm and put everyone on lockdown, which would have only postponed the inevitable retaliation.

This was a convict-code issue, and rules are rules. Andre went to the brothers who had lost the money and asked for a twenty-four-hour delay in their response. Then he went to the party who had taken the money and reasoned with them. The convict code says if a brother wants your stuff and challenges you for it, then you must fight to protect it. If you're not willing to fight, then you lose your property. However, if someone comes in and steals your belongings while you are not in your cell, then the brothers will help you get it back. It's an honor thing. So, Andre reasoned with them that this was the same, only on a bigger scale. They must obey the code. The council worked it out so there would be no retaliation, as long as the gang who got the money back did not boast about it. It would remain a private transaction, and that's exactly what happened.

So, Andre arranged for the $3,000 to be safely returned to those it belonged to. The Peace Council averted what could have been a bloody war that would have threatened the lives of not only inmates, but correctional officers as well. Andre had used his considerable influence to keep the peace with his deliberate actions and carefully constructed words. If he had been careless and shot from the hip—or worse, escalated the situation with reckless language—things could have spun out of control. Peace was on the move once again, and we saw that these men have the ability and the power to police themselves if properly motivated.

6) *When Wrong, Promptly Admit It and Make Amends*

We live in a world where admitting you are at fault is viewed as weakness. We see politicians deny to the death, only to have them admit their wrongdoings in humiliation after they've been caught. Then they lose all credibility, or at least what they had. We also see some parents doing the same thing with their kids, rarely admitting when they make mistakes but staying on the offensive as the one in charge and shutting children down with their authority. When kids are shut down, they tend to act out.

When in a debate or a disagreement, I have found it is an effective strategy to give the other side a point every now and then, as long as it is genuine. Think about how you feel when someone sincerely apologizes or admits you were right when you are engaged in a conflict. Do you lose respect for them? Actually, the opposite often holds true. I tend to gain respect for you when you are big enough to concede a point and admit you are mistaken. It brings an energy into the discussion that is positive and constructive. On the other hand, when someone is clearly in the wrong, but stubbornly refuses to give any ground, then I lose respect for them, as it speaks to their integrity or lack thereof. If your aim is to be right, regardless of the facts, then you will drive away your opponents, making it impossible to come to a resolution. However, if I behave honorably and admit when I am wrong, and if I am willing to change my mind, then I will win my rival's respect and possibly be in a position to move him closer to my position.

Once again, all this takes is humility, which is a strength of powerful leaders.

This is a crucial point in our nation's history. We need our leaders to find their humility and come together on the issues dividing our country. What if one were willing to admit when they were in error? What if the other were willing to concede a point as well? Can you imagine the energy that would create? It is weak and insecure to refuse to admit a mistake or a weakness. We expect our kids to do it, yet we can't even get our leaders to practice the same. This is a time for radical humility and dangerous unselfishness. If neither side is willing to concede anything, then we have no hope of reconciliation. We have created a climate wherein the thinking is, "When you lose, I win. And when you win, I lose." This is a miserable strategy for failure. We're all right sometimes, and we're all wrong sometimes. The truly strong and secure are not afraid to admit weakness. When you win, I win, and when you lose, I lose. Every time.

The Enforcer's Repentance

I was speaking at an event in Grand Rapids, Michigan, and the speaker after me was Mary Berghuis, a warden over two prisons in the Midwest. Miss Mary, as I called her, would eventually serve fifty years for the Department of Corrections in her state and retire as their longest-standing employee. She would also become a trusted friend and advisor to me. I enjoyed what she had to say, and we later met. She asked if I would be willing to help with gang violence at her level-four high-security prison. She said they had been experiencing a rash of attacks between the Bloods and other groups. When recruiting or retaliating, they were issuing "Buck-Fifties." This practice is brutal. The victim is held down and a razor, which has been burned into a plastic comb, is used to slice all the way from mouth to ear. It takes 150 stitches to heal the wound. This scar is forever a sign that this man is a snitch, and he will carry that mark for life, even if he hasn't necessarily snitched. It's a way for the Bloods to use fear to recruit more members into their gang.

So, we set it up, and she chose 150 men to participate. At the launch I asked the deputy warden of security who the major players were as we looked across the gym at all the men coming in and being seated. I wanted to know who the power players were so I could make my way to them during breaks and build rapport. There was a bald, white brother sitting in the very back with a big guy beside him, obviously there to protect him. The deputy warden said, "See the white guy in the back with his enforcer next to him? Get him. He's got a lot of pull." He was not an easy guy to get, as the white-supremacy gangs are tough to penetrate in most prisons. However, I eventually won his respect, and he did so well that he ended up being chosen to share at the graduation celebration. But it would be his enforcer who made a lasting impact on me.

Two months later, after a spirited graduation celebration, the enforcer waited in line to speak to me. Enforcers are more than just bodyguards; they are the heavy guys sent to "take care of things." It might be to collect a debt, rough somebody up (or worse), send a message, or go to war. This guy was definitely a warrior, and he was intimidating to look at. I certainly wouldn't want him to come and see me.

We hadn't interacted much throughout the process because he was quiet and kept to himself for the most part. He was large, strong, and tatted up, and he bore the scars that told me he had done some pretty hard time. He was doing a life sentence, so he didn't have much to lose if he was sent to put in some work. As we spoke, his eyes filled with tears and his lip began to quiver, which was odd in a place like this from a man like him. He said, "I just wanted to let you know your program saved a life." I replied that I knew this program saves lives in many places. He corrected me: "No, I mean it saved the life of someone in this gym."

I asked if he wanted to elaborate, and he continued, "A couple of weeks ago an order was given, and I was the one this work was given to, because that's what I do." He went on, "I was on my way across the yard to this man's unit, and I was going to kill him. When I got to the dorm, I was about to enter, and then I looked down and saw this damn wristband. I thought to myself, 'I cannot dishonor the brothers of POPP.' So I turned around and headed back across the compound to my building, thinking to myself that I would go back to my bunk, take off the wristband, and then I would go back and do him. But that walk across the yard gave me time to think, and it began to bother me. I went back to my people and asked them to reconsider, in light of everything we were learning. Believe it or not, they agreed. I just wanted to thank you." The order was overturned, and a member of the POPP squad is still breathing.

This was such a significant interaction, and it meant so much to me. He had practiced this crucial step in the heat of the battle and corrected a wrong before he even made it. I am proud of him, and this gives me even more hope. When wrong, promptly admit it and make amends. Who knew it would end up saving a life? Perhaps it has saved many. It is never weak to admit a wrong and make it right. Just ask the enforcer.

7) *Treat Your Opponent with Dignity and Respect, Especially When You Disagree*

I made a decision long ago that <u>I was going to treat everyone with the same respect, whether they earned it or not.</u> As a matter of fact, those who get the least respect from the world deserve more of mine, because they are starved for it, and I believe in feeding hungry people. If I show the utmost respect to the man under the bridge, or the convict, or the crack addict, or the prostitute, then I am projecting compassion and grace onto the least of these, and whatever I project onto you comes right back at me. This is a universal law.

Brothers in prisons are often surprised when I treat them the same way, or even better, than I would a famous pastor or a successful CEO. The wealthy and famous don't need as much respect because people are always falling over one another to get close to them. The least of us, as Jesus called them, crave respect because they rarely, if ever, receive it. When you show respect to the unrespectable, they never forget it and will quickly become your ally. However, it must be genuine, because these brothers can spot a fraud a mile away, and you rarely get a second chance with them.

Men need respect; our Creator designed us this way. When a man feels disrespected, it either drives him further into his insecurity, or it drives him to retaliate. In a prison, respect is everything. The convict code is built on it: how to earn it, how to keep it, how to lose it, and what to do when you don't receive it. If I can't gain the prisoners' respect, then I will lose credibility and be ineffective, and possibly even find some trouble.

Disagreements are inevitable between men, especially when they live in close quarters in a stress-filled environment. The problem is that men typically have only two ways to handle it: to fight or to run, but running away is not a good option in a prison because you can't really hide behind the wire. So, the question becomes, how do you handle disagreements and conflict when they find you? If we don't change the code in terms of respect, then violence will continue to mount, especially when times are tense.

Respect is about me, not about you. If I respect myself, then I will respect you. If I don't respect myself, then I can never truly respect you. I remember a Muslim leader getting up in front of all the brothers at one of our meetings years ago. This was an unusually tense time, as a war was spreading through all the state prisons between the Muslims and another powerful gang.

This man stood at the podium and said, "I am a proud Muslim, and I respect all of you. I respect you because of who I am, not because of who you are. I am a man of respect. Therefore, I will respect you, and I expect you to treat me with the same respect."

So, we teach the men to handle themselves respectfully, especially in the middle of a disagreement or an altercation. Can you keep your head when your opponent is losing theirs? Anyone can respect someone who poses no threat or is in a superior position. But the man who can act honorably, especially in the midst of a heated conversation, has the true power. Once again, I am reminded of Dr. King. He was hated and treated shamefully, but never sank to the level of his enemies. He said, "Let no man pull you so low as to hate him." So, Dr. King and other strong men who changed the world become the inmates' role models regarding how to handle a disagreement. If I treat my enemy with dignity and respect, especially when we disagree, this leaves the door open for future negotiation. However, if I treat my opponent disrespectfully during an altercation, then I might just have to watch my back forever, as I could have created an enemy for life.

Trapped in a Van in Tijuana

I was originally invited to Tijuana to facilitate our Forty Days to Freedom program at La Mesa prison. So, I had my publisher translate one of my books into Spanish, and our program went amazingly well, even with the language barrier. I was going to Tijuana so often that I became comfortable in that dangerous city, even though I stand out and nobody down there looks like me these days. Tijuana has been caught in the middle of an intense war between rival cartels for several years, and it was intensifying at the time I began working there. Whoever controls the border between TJ and San Diego wins, as it is the most lucrative border crossing in the world. Drugs, guns, and humans are smuggled over, under, and through that border for billions of dollars a year. A new cartel has been formed by bringing together other splinter groups, and they are now challenging the cartel that has controlled that area for a long time. You might remember "El Chapo," who controlled that area for years. He was extradited to the US, and now leadership is unstable and vulnerable. It has become the murder capital of the world, and kidnappings are rampant.

Most times I cross that border alone because my buddy Jeff lives in San Diego and has a pass that allows him to drive through an express lane after he drops me off, and then he waits for me on the other side. One day after we had been working down in Terrazas, he dropped me off on the Mexico side and headed on across. As I walked down into the tunnel, I noticed it was a sea of humanity, and it would take hours for me to get across. I texted Jeff, and he told me to grab a taxi and head toward Otay, which is a smaller crossing about thirty minutes east of Tijuana. So, I headed out of the tunnel looking for a taxi driver. I must have looked like an easy mark as a tall, white American looking from side to side as if I were lost. I was in a hurry, tired, and a bit irritated, so I wasn't exactly in a state to make wise decisions. I teach the men the acronym HALT to help them remember to never make important decisions when they are **H**ungry, **A**ngry, **L**onely, or **T**ired. Well, I wasn't practicing what I preach, and things were about to get interesting.

I made eye contact with a man coming toward me, and I mouthed the words, "Are you a taxi driver?" He kind of nodded and kept coming. As he got closer, I said again, "Are you a taxi? I need to get to Otay as soon as I can."

He said, "Yeah, we'll get you across."

I told him I didn't need to get across, I needed to get to Otay. Once again, he said, "No worries, we'll get you across."

Impatient now, I ignored what he said, and replied, "Okay, but let's hurry. I need to get some money, unless you guys can swipe a card."

As we walked up the ramp, his partner pulled in beside us, but I didn't pay much attention to it. As we turned the corner, I looked up and saw a white panel van, to which I inquired, "Is that a taxi?" He nodded, and I attempted to get in. I couldn't get the door open, so he came and opened it for me. I jumped in and so did they, and we took off. I looked around and quickly assessed that this wasn't a taxicab, and these weren't taxi drivers. They were "coyotes." Coyotes get people across the border who can't get across by themselves. They're also the ones who smuggle people across, and I was getting more than a little worried.

A pit formed in my stomach as I realized this might be a situation. Kidnappings are rampant in Tijuana, and I had imagined this scenario every time I traveled west to go back down to this fascinating city. Maybe they were just hustlers, but I didn't know. When we reached the main road, I knew Otay would be to the left going east, but we went right. They became agitated at the traffic and cursed at the cars to let them in, while I sat quietly in the back of this sketchy van trying to figure out what was next. They pulled into a little store where they knew I could get some cash. They turned around to face me and said, "Now go get us the money."

The next words to come out of my mouth would be very important, but before I could think I just blurted out, "I can't!"

Their next question was surprising, as the driver replied, "Why not?"

I thought this was a fascinating question for hustlers to ask right in the middle of a hustle, or worse. Then I said, and I promise this is true, "Because it's not fair!" I know, I was surprised I said it too, but that's just what came out.

They looked at me, speechless, with a strange expression on their faces, and I continued, "You said you were a taxi, and you're not. You said you were taxi drivers, and you aren't. You said you would take me to Otay, and you didn't. Now if you take me to Otay, I will give you some of my money, but if you don't, I just can't! You're honorable men, I know that, and you know it wouldn't be right to take my money without doing what you said you would do. Now do the right thing and let me out of this van."

I tried to get the door open, but it wouldn't budge. They just stared at me, and I turned up the volume a bit, as I was getting more anxious. "Come on now. You need to let me out of this damn van!"

At this, the man on the passenger side inexplicably got out, wrestled my door open, and let me out. I didn't run, but I walked with purpose toward a yellow car that said TAXI. The two men followed me and blocked the car I was trying to get into, because the driver wouldn't let me in. After I pleaded, he unlocked the door, and we drove right around them as they cursed the driver. The ride to Otay was completely silent, as my new friend was quite upset that I had involved him in my drama.

To this day, I am not sure what their intentions were, but I do know things might have gone a lot differently if I wasn't accustomed to hanging around shady characters. My brothers behind the wire have taught me so many things I'm not even aware of. They taught me how to deal with a man respectfully while communicating with my eyes that I am someone who deserves to be respected. They taught how to keep my head in dangerous situations and not lose my cool. They taught me how to use my language in a way that diffuses a situation rather than pouring gas on the flames. Basically, they taught me how to use my energy to control a situation that is escalating, and I am forever grateful. I had unknowingly practiced the principle of treating my enemies with dignity and respect, especially when we disagree. I believe this disagreement was handled peacefully because those men felt respected.

In the next act we will look at the collective dream of our brothers behind the wire, and how they might have the answers to some of the problems we are facing. Then we will discuss some of the solutions we've found together.

The POPP Brothers at La Mesa Prison in Tijuana

Act Two

THE STORY OF ROOTS

My Partner Roots

If you ever see me on stage delivering a keynote presentation, whether it be at a corporate event, in a prison, or at a school or church, you will most likely meet my partner, "Roots." Roots is what you would call a walking stick, a cane, or a staff. However, he is fundamentally a branch that fell from a tree. I named him Roots in honor of the one who made him for me.

In 2013 I began working the streets in a tough neighborhood in Downtown Atlanta. We were helping the homeless and at-risk youth. This happens to be the number-one incarceration zip code in Georgia, and it sits less than a mile away from the Atlanta Federal Penitentiary. The greatest risk for these kids is crime, violence, and incarceration. Youth gangs are rampant, and the pull is strong for these kids who are dropping out, hitting the streets, and practicing going to prison.

I met a homeless brother on those streets, and we became fast friends. He would help us, and we would put a little money in his pocket or give him a warm place to sleep in the church we were using. He was in his thirties, happened to be black, and was born in Jamaica. He was going through a rough stretch and living in a little tent not far from the building where we were serving. One day the city bulldozed his tent, and he had no place to stay. He always had a cool decorative walking stick with him, and I learned this was his hustle and one of the ways he supported himself. He would always say to me, "Brother Kit, you need a stick!" I asked him why, and he replied, "If you're going to work these streets, then you're going to need protection." So, I asked where I could acquire such a stick, and he told me not to worry; he would hook me up.

About a week later he presented me with my very own staff. It was beautiful. He cut the branch down to size, whittled and shaved it, carved grooves in it, painted it, and then weatherproofed it. He even put my POPP symbol on it. I named it Roots in honor of its designer, because that's my friend's name. Then my brother moved on, and I lost contact with him. I often wonder if he knows his special gift has become somewhat famous and has a following of its own. Recently I received a request from a Division I college basketball team asking, "Is Roots available on March seventh?" They love having him on the bench for good luck. The high school kids love him too. He's helped three of our POPP football teams win state championships; they touch him for luck when they come out of the tunnel. Two of those teams have given me state championship rings, which I treasure. You never know what one random act of kindness can do, as this unseen homeless brother is impacting the world without even knowing it.

I have held my cane in the air and asked this question in prisons, schools, corporations, and churches: "What's his name?" And the crowd yells, "Roots!" And then I ask the second question: "What does he mean?" And they shout, "Potential!" I've asked that question all over the world, as Roots has become a symbol of realized potential. This broken branch has gone on a world tour. I began to imagine the journey of this fallen branch. There was a time when he thrived atop a hundred-year-old oak tree. He was living the life—sunshine, cool breeze, nourishing sap, birds perched, and refreshing rain. Then something knocked him out of his purpose, and he was separated from the life he was created to live. Maybe it was a storm, or maybe a lightning strike, or an axe, but something knocked him down and out.

So, there he lay, flat on his back, trampled on, kicked aside, and destined to be burned, because that's what we do with trash. But then a homeless brother saw him, and more importantly, saw him for what he *could* be. He cleaned him up and designed him for a specific purpose, which was for my protection. Little did he know this nasty, broken branch would have thousands of people shouting his name. He became a symbol to kids of what they could be, especially after the storms.

The brothers behind the wire love Roots because they relate to falling flat and losing everything, destined to be thrown away and forgotten. Through our program we see them the way they could be, and the way their Creator designed them to be. They represent raw potential realized, and they become an inspiration to kids. That is a dream that is bigger than themselves, and one that can pull them through hard times. It is the powerful pull of a daring dream.

Andrew Fuller, a.k.a. Roots, was killed on December 27, 2020, by a drunk driver while coming home from work on his scooter. Rest in peace, Brother Roots. You changed my life forever.

Chapter Four
WHERE ARE THE DREAMERS?

We are living in a day and age where true dreamers are becoming more and more rare. As conflict, violence, and hatred erupt on the streets, as a global pandemic rages and a nation is gripped with fear, as the economy is tumbling and many are out of work, the dreams of many are growing cold and dying on the vine. When dreams die for the parents and guardians, the young suffer because they don't learn how to dream. They become so disillusioned with the older generation that they simply live in today and don't dream of a better tomorrow.

If ever there was a time in our nation's history when we need dreamers, it is now. Many are comparing this time in our country with the sixties: a time of revolution, upheaval, and social unrest. The difference? The sixties were inspired by dreamers such as Dr. King, Mr. Mandela, Malcolm X, Rosa Parks, John and Bobby Kennedy, Maya Angelou, Bob Marley, Cesar Chavez, Rabbi Heschel, Thich Nhat Hanh, and many others. We had courageous, nonviolent role models to light the way for young generations. However, America killed the dreamers and took away their voices. The nation turned to violence for solutions, many concluding that nonviolence is not the answer. Haters can kill the dreamers, but they can't kill the dream.

So, we are a generation who has turned to other things for comfort rather than peace, and settled for selfish, worldly dreams rather than world-changing visions. Where are all the dreamers today? What if they are hiding behind miles and miles of razor wire across the Land of the Free? What if they find the solutions we seek? What if they are just waiting for a noble dream and the tools to carry it out? Why can't they dream a dream that will awaken a sleeping nation? It turns out they can, and they are, but nobody has been watching. Until now.

Broken Branches

Halfway through sharing about my partner, Roots, the brothers realize they are the broken branches who have fallen to the ground. They are the ones who have been discarded, hidden away, and treated like trash. There was a time when things were different for them, even if they have to go back to when they were little boys. Most of them grew up poor; a lot of them were abused; many were abandoned and taken in by the gangs; many were latchkey kids with no supervision or real parenting. They didn't choose to be born into that life. However, that is not an excuse for criminal behavior. We all must answer to a higher power for our choices.

Their crimes come from many different situations. Some were crimes of desperation. Others were crimes of passion, while others were crimes of revenge or self-defense. The majority of their crimes involve alcohol or drugs, and are directly related to addiction and drug-seeking behavior. Many of them were victims of systematic abuse and became abusers themselves. Others hit the streets when they were young in order to get away, or because they had no one capable of raising them. A large number of them grew up in the foster-care system, and still others chose the streets rather than a dangerous home situation. Approximately a third of them struggle with some sort of mental illness. These are not excuses, just the facts.

When incarcerated, they became the fallen branch destined to be thrown away as trash. Many of them had a decent life before their fall, and then they were disconnected from their life source from all the various situations listed above. They were piled into a heap and dumped in a place where no one has to see them or hear from them again. What if we provided them with treatment and care? What if nonviolent offenders were offered drug and alcohol recovery first, before being thrown away? What if we built more recovery centers, where felons could be mandated by the courts to get help with addiction and anger management? What if they had access to mental health care and therapy, rather than being thrown behind the wire for years and years with the truly violent ones, only to learn to be better criminals?

There are alternatives. We could easily fix our current broken model if we reappropriated some of the $80 billion that will be spent on corrections in the US this year alone. A portion of that money could be used for treatment, care, recovery, and therapy. We could stop building more prisons, start shutting down some of the ones we already have, and build more schools and rehab facilities.

Just imagine, we could empty the prisons while also making our communities safer. However, that would mean the prison industrial complex would lose some of the billions in profit they will earn this year from locking up poor people. It's all about the bottom line, rather than the broken branches. Approximately 97 percent of the brothers behind the wire are coming home someday. The question is, in what condition will they return?

Just like Roots, they found themselves on their backs until someone saw them for who they could be. A nasty broken branch was cleaned up, given a purpose, and sent on a mission to inspire the hopeless. That's exactly what happens through the Power of

Peace Project. We *see* them. We *feel* them. And we send them out to be an inspiration to the kids who are not listening to anyone else. A homeless brother saw the branch for what it could be, and that transformed it. Over all these years I have been seeing these broken brothers for what they could be, and that has made all the difference. They long to be connected to the tree, the Tree of Life.

The Powerful Pull of a Daring Dream

There is a principle in the universe: The big thing always pulls the small thing. The black hole pulls the stars, the sun pulls the earth, the earth pulls the moon, the moon pulls the tides, the tides pull the ocean, the ocean pulls the river, the river pulls the stream, the stream pulls the creek, the creek pulls the pond, and the pond is fed by the clouds. The fascinating circle of life goes on. The smaller thing always gets pulled by the bigger thing, and the smaller thing never needs to push. Nature just goes with the flow as it gets pulled along by life. Nature never resists universal laws and principles. And then there are humans.

Now more than ever, we need to stay focused on our dreams. When we design a dream bigger than ourselves, the law kicks in and the big thing pulls the small thing. A big dream can pull you through obstacles, distractions, failures, temptations, and even your fears.

Do you ever feel like you're pushing your way through life rather than being pulled by it? That way of living is unsustainable long term and typically leads to burnout. It's time to raise up a new generation of dreamers, and that is what we do with young people in our POPP programs. They learn to design big dreams that have great value, and we always protect what we value. Then it's simply a matter of learning how to protect those dreams from dream killers and from those who hate on dreamers, because they have no vision of their own. The bigger the dream, the stronger the pull.

Dreams are dangerous in a prison. These men have been beaten down by life and have lowered their standards to a point where mere survival is the goal. Basic needs like food, water, and protection become the primary focus, and dreams die over time. I challenge them to dream again and dare them to resurrect hope. There is resistance to this challenge at first, but the commitment is only for forty days, and I reason with them that they can do anything for forty days. Forty days, I teach them, is enough to break unhealthy habits and create new ones. They are encouraged to keep their dreams to themselves if need be, but in no time many of them want to share their dreams with the group, even with their rivals. I give them a guarantee: If this program does not change you, then I'll be happy to refund you your pain and misery at the end of the campaign!

Their dream can be anything that is bigger than themselves and that carries great value. Some dream of getting out someday and going home to help their kids. Others dream of learning a trade or earning a degree behind the wire. Some dream of finding love again in the free world and learning how to love someone more than they love themselves. Still others dream of getting out and establishing a nonprofit organization to help clean up the mess they made on the streets. In a Mexican prison, one of the brothers shared that his dream was to see the ocean for the first time and open his own deep-sea fishing company.

If they dare to dream again, then naturally it's harder to hate on the dreams of their rivals. Once again, they are finding commonality and walking in one another's shoes. The logical next step is helping them support and protect their brothers' dreams, not just their own. The POPP peace movement shifts into overdrive when they develop a collective dream to change their environment and create "better time" for the entire prison. They then find the kind of respect that is much more powerful than what the convict code promises.

Dangerous Dreamers

When I met these men behind the wire for the first time, I happened to be in a dreamless season of life. Little did I know these brothers would help birth the biggest dream I've ever had, at least as far as my life's work goes. I didn't find my dream; it found me. Dreams are like that—oftentimes they're hiding, just waiting to reveal themselves when you become available. I was so hungry for a dream to replace the one I'd lost, and it was inevitable that one would find me. What I seek is always seeking me.

A dream is dangerous because you are setting yourself up to have your heart broken, and nobody wishes for that kind of pain. It's easier to harden your heart. I found that a broken heart is not so bad after all. Heartbreaks are a part of life, but if I must get my heart busted up again, let it be because I was bold enough to chase a big vision. I'd rather get a broken heart than have my heart slowly grow cold over time because I was afraid to chase my dreams and settled for so much less than I was capable of.

Dreamers get out front, and nobody wants to be out front in a prison. The goal is to stay out of the spotlight and fly under the radar as much as possible. If you have a big dream and someone else doesn't, then they will not only hate on your dream, but they might try to keep you from realizing it. When men are preparing to go home as they get closer to their release date, they typically don't let anyone know, because those who aren't going home don't want you to go either. They might even try to sabotage your release and force you to catch a new charge and get more time. So, dreamers are rare, and those who live out a public dream are exceptional. POPP resurrects dreams, and then more and more men have the courage to follow theirs as well.

As my dream came back to life, I inspired those around me to dream as well. Those first twelve men who signed our first peace pledge dreamed a collective dream and unknowingly changed the course of many lives. They learned from the great dreamers like Gandhi, King, and Mandela, and they became inspired. That inspiration is the spark that can set the whole prison on fire with faith. Maybe they will show us the way in the free world to dream once again. POPP is not a program, but a movement for dreamers.

A Young Brother's Big Dream

I am standing on a stage in 2013 at a POPP graduation celebration in a Michigan prison. The mood is lively and festive, as the brothers have just made their presentations, performed, and received their well-deserved certificates of achievement. I am saying my goodbyes and encouraging the men, when a young brother walks up to me. "Brother Kit," he says, "can I ask you a question?" I tell him of course he can, and he continues, "This program has changed my life and made such a huge difference in this prison. I've never seen anything like it. Here is my question—do you believe there is a Nobel Peace Prize in this for us?" I'm speechless, and my eyes begin to well up. Here is a twenty-one-year-old inmate doing time in a tough prison with an idea so big it stops me in my tracks.

In just forty short days, this kid came to believe that maybe, just maybe, he and the brothers can change the world so much they can be worthy of the Nobel. I get goosebumps just writing these words. This young man already had a greater vision for this crazy movement than I did. I tell him, "I'm not sure, brother, but

I can promise you this—I will never stop fighting for all of you to be worthy of one, and some day, years from now, maybe we'll stand together on a stage in Norway and accept one for all your brothers behind the wire."

He enhanced my vision and gave me another mountain to climb. Prayerfully, one day my brothers and sisters behind the wire will earn one, as more and more of them across the country catch a huge dream like this young dreamer did. They want to change the world, and perhaps they will. Dr. King would be so proud of them.

Chapter Five
THE ANTIVIRUS

POPP Brothers Take a Stand in Ohio

Currently we're in the middle of a global pandemic, and the race is on to find an effective vaccine. Our nation is spending vast amounts of money, resources, and human capital to protect the vulnerable among us. What if we spent a fraction of that same time, money, and energy and aimed it at changing our prison system to eradicate the disease of violence that is plaguing our communities? What if we invested heavily in developing programs for true rehabilitation for the two-million-plus who are locked up? They are being released in droves, hungry, angry, and destined to reoffend in our communities. Many are not even afraid to go back, and some actually choose it because they have been institutionalized. Crime and violence are also a pandemic, and we desperately need a vaccine.

The solution for the flu is created by the virus itself. The solution for a snakebite is created by the venom. So, what is the answer for crime and violence in America? Transformed criminals who have been inoculated. They carry the disease but have built up an immunity, just like with vaccines. Who better to go back as returning citizens, no longer convicts, to become role models, becoming the men they always dreamed they could be? The antivirus carries a viral load of the disease, enough for the body to recognize it and create the immunity it needs to quarantine and delete it. These men carry the disease, but having been cured, they are now inoculated. They know the game, they have the code, and they know the streets. They're wise to the ways of the world, but they have overcome it.

Kids are impressionable, so we must give them new impressions. For many of them, they have always wanted a father figure in their lives. We can start there. Mentoring programs are crucial, but the truth is many of these misguided young men will never listen to anyone other than those who understand the streets, because they speak their language and have earned their respect. Today's youth need a new code to live by, and a standard by which to operate. Without mentors to teach them, they have simply created their own code. The problem is that their code is sending many of them to prison, where they will repeat the sins of their elders. The principles these brothers behind the wire helped me to create have served me in the free world, in all the dangerous places I've operated. That's why I believe it will work on the streets too, not just behind those walls. These kids desperately need the antivirus and the *new* convict code. A code built on the foundation of mutual respect, integrity, and loyalty.

What is missing in many of our communities is the strong male role model. Many of these kids are raising themselves, and often choose the quickest and easiest way to get what they want. Where are the strong brothers who are supposed to be raising these kids? They make up the growing army behind the wire. The War on Drugs campaign and "tough on crime" legislation has made it easy pickings for minorities and poor people. Locking up men on nonviolent drug charges has filled up our prisons, which has been good for business and for the bottom line of the correctional system.

However, the ones who have been the most affected by this dysfunctional system are the youth in our inner-city, suburban, and rural communities. No one is immune. There is a void in the heart of our neighborhoods where strong men are supposed to be raising strong young men. You might be saying, "This is their own fault. They should pull themselves up by their bootstraps." I would ask you to imagine growing up in an area that is below the poverty line, where there is little hope for quality education or a way out. We're talking about generational poverty, a cycle that is difficult to break without real support. Many of these kids have never even seen someone hold down a job, much less get a degree. It's hard to imagine something you've never seen.

The answer to crime and violence is transformed criminals. They are the only voice that many of these tough kids will listen to. Their elders who have been there and done that already have credibility and influence; they just need to utilize it. These brothers behind the wire are more willing to *be* the change than anyone in the free world knows, and they are responding to that challenge. I am getting more and more calls all the time from brothers who have gotten out and now want to answer the call and help the kids. How did they get my contact info? It's on the back of many of my books that are scattered across America, and now they are reaching out. They believe they are the solution. It's time to ask them to assist us.

Ask Them for Help

The first step is awareness. The nation needs to see what's going on behind the razor wire. People need to be appalled and the conscience of the nation needs to be awakened. Right now, no one sees the horrors, hears the screams in the night, witnesses the violence, or knows of the police brutality. It is time for them to see. Second, prison officials all the way up to the governors need to be pressured to find alternatives to the current model, which is built to fail. That is the only way this broken system can change. We must apply pressure to our elected officials. Thirdly, we must get the brothers behind the walls to help us. No one has thought of this approach because they don't believe they can, or don't believe they want to. I know different; I have seen it work too many times to be skeptical. They have proven to me time and time again that they are not only willing to help, but they are motivated to help, and are very capable of bringing about radical change. If we develop an effective vaccine for COVID-19, we will surely share it with the world. If we discover the antivirus to crime and violence, we should also share it with the world. They carry the crime virus, but they have been cured.

I do not believe we can reform the prison system without help from the residents. They have the power, the influence, and the means to change it. We just need to provide them with the hope, the inspiration, and the tools to help them help themselves, which is exactly what they want. I believe this: People will live up to or down to the way we see them. If we treat them like animals, they will bite. If we treat them like honorable men, most times they will not disappoint us. Even if they are not interested in changing, they still tend to act respectfully if we simply see them as human beings. The same is true with us in the free world. We tend to level up or level down to people's expectations of us. It's time. The brothers behind the wire are ready, willing, and able. Just ask them.

Criminal Gangs Anonymous

In 2016, Jeff Wadstrom, who founded the nonprofit Bridge to

the Future, reached out to me and asked if I would be willing to take my program into La Mesa prison in Tijuana. Many of the kids they work with have fathers who are locked up there, and that was the reason for his request. The program went extremely well, and I continued to go back. I went to San Diego and down into Tijuana every month for over a year to learn what they were doing so effectively with the kids so I could replicate it in the States. They were saving kids' lives, and continue to do so today.

Jeff has a good friend named Mike Slater who hosts a popular nationally syndicated radio talk show out of San Diego. Mike is a regular contributor to Fox News, CNN, Headline News, and other news outlets, and was named "Top Five Rising Stars" in talk radio. I've been a guest on Mike's show eight times now, so we have become good friends.

Donovan State Prison, just outside of San Diego, invited us to come inside and work with a group called Criminal Gangs Anonymous. This is a type of support group for gang members who are attempting to leave the life and fly straight, but that can be a dangerous thing to do. The meetings look like something out of a Danny Trejo movie, with a fascinating group of characters. You see tats, bandanas, sunglasses, and muscles. When you look around the room, you see gang members from all the different sets, but they all have one thing in common: They are trying to leave the gang life in a place where that can get you killed.

So, on one of my radio interviews with Mike I said, "You should go with us into the prison sometime."

He replied, "I don't think my pregnant wife would let me!"

Over the coming weeks I kept on him until he agreed, as I promised him it would change his life. On my next trip the following month, we set it up. When the day for our prison event finally arrived, Mike was more excited than nervous after all the times he had heard me tell stories about these amazing men behind the wire. The first time you go into a prison, you never forget it. I told Mike I might put him on the spot to speak to the men, and he said he didn't think so! We entered the room and began to meet and greet. The brothers were excited to meet a radio celebrity, but I think he was even more excited to meet them.

After I finished my message, I invited Mike to come up and take the stage. He is comfortable in front of audiences, so he didn't hesitate. What he did next was touching, heartfelt, and brilliant. He began to tell them about the upcoming birth of his first child, a son. His wife was eight months pregnant, so he was somewhat anxious. He shared with them that this was his first child and that he was nervous about raising a son in this crazy world. Then he surprised them, and me, as he asked them to give him some advice. It was so sincere, and the men were eager to help. The fathers began to share one by one and offer him counsel. One brother said, "Make sure you never beat him." Another added, "Make sure you spend time with him." Then another brother shared, "Tell him that you love him." Still another said, "Don't ever leave him." And then one of the brothers in blue said, "When you wrap him up in his blanket, do it like this—make him like a little burrito, but not too tight." It was magical, as these men were trying to help him not make the mistakes they had made with their sons. They truly do care.

Nobody was joking; they were very serious. Our sacred time together brought laughter, goosebumps, and tears as these hard men shared advice with a celebrity from the free world and he gladly, and humbly, accepted it. He told them that one day, when his son asks him where he learned to be such a good father, he would tell him former gangsters in a maximum-security prison taught him how to treat his son. Once again, I was reminded that these hated, feared, and forgotten men aren't necessarily who the free world thinks they are.

Gangster Party

A Peaceful Gangster Party in Atlanta

In 2014, I got a call from a number I didn't recognize. I picked up anyway. The voice on the other end, in a hushed tone, said, "Brother Kit, it's Dre."

I said, "Dre who?"

He replied, "It's your brother Andre."

I said, "Hey, brother, are you out?" I was surprised because this brother was doing a life sentence, and he was calling from a cell phone.

He said, "No, not really."

I told him we had to hang up and I couldn't communicate with him like this.

He said, "Before you go, I've got to tell you something really quick. I need you to be Downtown on the West End Sunday at two o'clock p.m." He gave me the address and said, "Can I count on you, bro?" I told him he could and asked what it was. He told me I would find out when I got there, and then he said goodbye.

I didn't know what to think. Was it a church service or a service project? Was it a community event or a family reunion? Or, maybe it was a fundraiser or political rally. I was curious and couldn't wait to find out, because this brother is trustworthy, and he really wanted me to go. So, on Sunday I headed down to the West End of Atlanta to an underserved and tough community. I had never been to this neighborhood, and when I got to the address, I didn't see a park or a church; there was no ball field or community center. It was a corner barber shop, and the parking lot was full. There was gangster rap blaring and heavy smoke billowing from a barbecue pit. There were Muslim messages blasting from a speaker, and it was a colorful crowd. All men, and the brothers were wearing red, blue, or black; some wore a fez, and others wore skull caps. It turns out I had rolled up on a genuine gangster party.

This was a group of five rival gangs having a cookout with a solidarity march following the party. There were Crips, Bloods, Gangster Disciples, Moors (a sect of Islam), and the Nation of Islam. There was food, music, laughter, and no edge whatsoever. At certain times everybody would throw up their gang signs in a big group and laugh. I have never seen anything like it since the nineties, when there was a short truce between rival gangs in South Central LA following the riots. Dre had told me to look for a large brother in red named Mike, and he was easy to find.

I made my way to him and said, "Are you Big Mike?"

He said, "Yeah," in a low bass tone.

I said, "Dre sent me."

He looked up and said, "Are you Kit?" Then he gave me a big bear hug and began introducing me around. I met the leaders of each group and we took some pictures. It was like I was a "made man," and they were so hospitable and generous.

Mike said, "You want to march with us?"

To which I replied, "I love to march, Big Mike!"

So, everyone gathered around, and he began to rally the troops. He introduced me to the whole group as everyone began picking up their signs. I had no idea why we were marching; I was just thrilled to be at the party. Five rival gangs marched together in solidarity against police brutality, and it was absolutely peaceful. I shook Mike's hand and thanked him for including me. Another bear hug, and that was the last I've seen of him. However, one of the group pics that was taken became their organizational poster, and one guy stood out: a tall brother of less color throwing up a peace sign with a black "Power of Peace" T-shirt. I learned later that the Georgia Bureau of Investigation was watching. It is a day I will never forget.

Here's the kicker: The whole rally was organized from behind the wire. Do you see the power and influence they have? They are connected to the streets—as a matter of fact, many leaders are running things on the streets from the prisons based on their rank. Can you imagine if prison gangsters became peacemakers and began using their considerable influence on the streets? This is an army of potential world-changers just waiting to make a difference. You can say, "How do we know they won't use their influence to cause more trouble?" My answer is they're already doing that. It's time for them to call different shots.

Now it's time to give them the tools and the motivation to change things, and all they need is a new code. In their world, reputation is everything. When I get them to imagine their lasting legacy if they were the ones who began a movement of peace and nonviolence on the streets, they're curious. They've just never been asked to help. Like you, it's hard for them to believe it's possible at first, but I just told you a story where they had already started doing it. If we offer them a better life, many of them will take it, if we simply show them how. They are ready to go back and fix up what they tore up, and teach these dangerous kids a new code—the POPP code.

It's Time for a Change

The wardens love our program because it addresses one of their biggest threats. The officers love our program because the inmates behave better with fewer assaults on the men and women in black. The prisoners love our program because they earn a better quality of life with more privileges, which makes them feel more like free men. Their families love our program because their loved ones are in a safer environment, will come home sooner with fewer mental health and behavioral problems, and, prayerfully, they will never go back. However, many of our elected officials fear these types of programs because they are unconventional and out-of-the-box. It's time for governors and commissioners to consider new approaches and fresh ideas to fix this broken system.

The current system works for those in charge because it is much easier to lock inmates down when they break the rules than it is to bring them together in unity and peace. Plus, nobody has ever seen it done on a large scale, and we tend to fear what we do not know. Our current system rarely rehabilitates residents, and only serves to create more violence. I am by no means saying those who run the prisons want violence in their institutions, but we know violence is increasing, and more and more brothers are being released in a worse condition than when they went in. This punitive model is predictable, but with no incentives or rewards built in, it is destined to fail. Whatever we resist, we strengthen. Dr. King said, "Darkness cannot drive out darkness, only light can. Hatred cannot drive out hate, only love can." Our current system uses violence to end violence, and that is ineffective and unsustainable. We must find a better way.

Chapter Six
THE CONVICT CODE

In the prison system there is a code, a system, a standard operating procedure. You don't decide whether you want to play this game; you have no choice. It's a matter of how fast you can learn and survive in the process. There's no manual or list of rules; it's just the nature of the beast, a way of living and way of dying. It's the way you conduct business, the way you handle conflicts, the way you look at each other, and the way you don't look at each other. It's how you handle information, how you deal with staff, and how you deal with disrespect. It's about consequences for actions and consequences for inaction. The code is predictable, and you better be ready at all times. Ignorance is no excuse; you are expected to learn. Most of these brothers learn the code on the streets and bring it into prison, but many others have never even heard of it, and must learn quickly or pay the price.

In many ways I respect these men who live by a code. I never really had a code of conduct growing up; I just followed my feelings and desires, and tried to avoid consequences. But these men have to live by a code, or they get hurt. So, I set out to learn the convict code, to respect the code, and to try to change the code. It's not a big leap from the old code to the new one; it just needs some additions and deletions, some edits and revisions. Convicts are the experts of their code, so who better to amend it and teach it to a young generation who is getting caught up in it?

The Wisdom of Sir Brown
Viewer Discretion Advised

Here is some inside intel about the code and life behind the wire from my brother Sir Brown, who is on the front lines of this good fight:

The convict code is basically a writ of distorted values, an upside-down doctrine for upside-down people. For the most part, we are a society of misfits. The unloved and unwanted. The world's rejects. In the free world, glancing at a person is nothing. Behind these walls, glancing at a person can cause you to lose your life. Saying "Good morning" can get you into an altercation. The normal reply is, "What's good about it?" Asking any type of question in the free world is fine. Asking questions could get your head split open. Borrowing money and not paying interest on it can cause an issue. Speaking too long in quiet with an officer draws suspicion. It's a good practice to have two or more witnesses within earshot of conversations with a staff member. Passing gas in a public area can get you hurt. If you're in your cell and have to pass gas (with your pants on), you sit on the toilet, pass gas, and flush simultaneously. Never share even the smallest amount of good news; this creates envy. Don't show photographs of attractive or influential people who support you; this creates jealousy. If you go to visit and someone asks how it was, even within your inner circle, just say it was okay.

This has more to do with withholding information from the staff. Someone falls out of a doorway with a razor slash across the face. The police ask everyone (including the victim), "Who did this?" The code says to be silent. Offer no clues, answer no questions. If you do give a reply, the only acceptable ones are, "I don't know," or "I didn't see." Even if the person dies. So, what about

The New Convict Code

the victim's family members? Do you give them clarity? Nope. No snitching at all. It's also a revenge game. If you survive an attack, the convict code says you must retaliate. If you give a name, the person could get transferred to another dorm or facility, and you may never be able to get them back.

The convict code is an odd thing. It is perfectly okay to walk into someone's cell and rob them for whatever they may have, as long as the person in the cell has an opportunity to defend what is his. But the convict code says you are breaking the code if you creep into someone's cell and steal. Sneak-stealing cannot be allowed. It's not tolerated in any dorm anywhere, the reason being the chaos it can cause. For example: You and I are at odds. We have a heated disagreement, and later that day you realize your watch is missing out of your locker. You have to use the process of elimination. Then you remember who you had a recent conflict with. You run up on me in an accusing tone. Everyone is watching, so my honor is even more at stake. I swing, and next thing you know we are both in the hole. You see, men will usually choose safety if no witnesses are around to tell the story. But usually, the way we respond is based on who is watching. Stealing is unacceptable also because the person who took the loss can decide to steal from someone else. Even a person whose reputation is beyond reproach. This creates a cycle that will reinvent itself for months or years.

There are basic similarities across prisons, with some shocking differences. Namely, homosexuality. Some prisons condone same-sex relationships. Some administrators use openly gay men as tools. If an inmate is violent and known to have gay tendencies, a supervisor may move a gay man into his cell. Gays can be used as rewards. Some affiliations turn a blind eye to homosexual activity if one of their members has been sentenced to a long prison term.

However, people getting raped daily is pure fiction. There are enough men who willingly choose that lifestyle. Of course, it happens, but that practice is frowned upon. Men don't come to prison and become gay. They were who they were before they got here. Once, a white dude wanted a cigarette badly. He said, "I will perform oral sex if someone gives me a cigarette." Truth is, he was craving the sex more than the nicotine and used the tobacco to give vent to his desires. It's damaging to your reputation as a man to keep the company of a homosexual. You have to have a strong reputation and witnesses overhearing your conversations.

Leaders, movers, and shakers must deal with everyone, so some interaction with those who are different is inevitable. If you are not interested in a homosexual relationship, it is unwise to ever have a gay man for a cellmate; you might be having sex before long. The gay person will be working on you from day one. If you're in the room with one, everyone will assume you are a couple. Do not let a gay man spend five minutes alone in your cell or the assumption will be made. Do not accept gifts or favors from anyone, especially a homosexual, unless you have no concerns about your reputation. If they deliver, provide information, assist with law work or tutoring, pay them. Pay their full price and don't ask for deals.

Throughout this journey I've learned many things. Most of them the hard way. Every important lesson I've learned came through pain and loss. In my early years as a kid, the strong were the ones in control, the ones with the best resources. Bullies and violent people controlled my small world. But a pattern seemed to emerge. The violent person usually met with an even more violent person. Bullies got bullied. And I realized all bullies are basically cowards. So, I knew I had to be strong. But being strong didn't mean I had to use violence to gain resources. I ran errands, had a paper route, took out the garbage for our apartment building. But also, I learned to box. I began at around ten or eleven years old. As my skill increased, the willingness for people to listen did too. The strong are given leeway.

I was the only son of my mother's four children. No dad in the home, so I was the man of the house. Girls argue. I settled their disputes with reason. This mindset followed me through school, through my teenage years of sports, and eventually into the crew I became a part of in my criminal life. I made efforts to always be reasonable. Even through extortion, I made it a point to leave a man with his dignity. Sounds crazy, but I'd say: "You cannot hustle around here without paying someone. It may as well be me. If you have an issue, you can call upon me and I will get it resolved." During my time in prison I committed violent acts in the early years. This gave people pause. But I tutored for free seven days a week almost from day one—a promise I made to my mother, who died while I was behind bars.

Violence causes more violence. It brings heat to your environment. Showers are cancelled or limited. Movement is cancelled or limited. Food is cancelled or limited. Yards, gym are cancelled or limited. Then comes the attention from the staff. Searching, taking, and destroying your property. What you gain from one violent act is lost a hundred times over by the repercussions. As a prison veteran, some respected men have a voice. Many of us use ours to bring peace, to resolve conflict, to lead, guide, and direct younger or just older misguided guys onto a better path. But without my violent history behind these walls, the job would have been far more difficult. A person gets robbed or beaten, then someone who is known to have once been a robber and a beater approaches the guy who committed the act. He says, "What you did was messed up. What if I take your stuff and beat you to sleep? You *wouldn't like it, would you? Knock it off, or your time is coming." Or, the once-violent person embraces the currently violent one and drops jewels on him, telling him stories of bullies who got their comeuppance, and suggesting he quit while he's ahead. I've tried both ways. The calm talk usually has a longer-lasting effect. And when possible, I slide some food their way to flip and create a little something for themselves.*

Georgia is one of only three states that offers no state pay. Meaning, in every other state in America, inmates are compensated for their labor. Especially in high-level, maximum-security facilities. Georgia pays nothing. Every compound has a factory that produces some product: clothes, soap, eyewear, mattresses, etc. If you refuse to work, you are given a write-up and a disciplinary form, and are subsequently charged five dollars for not going to work. Seems unfair, right? You don't get paid for going to work, but if you don't go, you have to pay the state. So, if a guy has no family support or doesn't have a skill like drawing portraits, he may resort to robbing or stealing, which only complicates matters. But there is a chain-gang slogan that is very popular: "If you're not feeding them, you can't tell them how to eat."

The Power of Collective Energy

As I went to serve in prisons more often, my energy began to change. My wife started noticing and getting worried. My language changed, my hair length changed, my clothing and shoes changed, the way I saw officers changed. Even my skin changed, as I began telling the POPP story on my arm in the form of tattoo art. The year was 2012, and I was in prison all the time. At least twice a week I was hanging out with gangsters and tough prisoners. The POPP movement was in full gear, and I was getting pretty good at the game. I had learned how to win the trust and respect of influential men behind the wire, and more and more prisoners were coming forward wanting to be a part of this young movement. They were learning from me, and I was learning from them. I was influencing them, but it turns out they were influencing me as well. It was a subtle thing that was happening, and I couldn't see it. I've been teaching kids for years that they have to be careful who they choose to be in their inner circle, because you will begin to become like them. Birds of a feather really do flock together. So I began to be much more deliberate and intentional about my visits and my inner circle of trusted inmates. We continued to influence each other, but it was with the intention of becoming stronger men. Iron sharpens iron, and we began to hold each other more accountable for the influence we had on one another.

This is an energy principle, and you can't get around it. Energy attracts like energy; this is how groups are formed. Whether it be a church or a gang, a corporation or a country club, we attract those who vibrate like us, and that attraction can be a strong pull. Prisons have a strong vibe, as there are as many as two thousand men living in close proximity and they are all energetically connected. All those individual frequencies create a "signature frequency" for that prison population. Once they learn they have the power to change that frequency, it becomes a game and we create momentum together. They learn they can shift the culture by utilizing their collective energy.

One of the first things I teach the inmates is the power of the mind and some fundamental principles of physics. When you break us down to our most basic elements, we are made out of pure energy. From cells to molecules, and atoms to quarks, we are energy beings. We are much more a wave than solid matter. The way our energy flows creates our signature frequency that we blast to the world. Everyone has a unique frequency, and we are literally bouncing into one another's frequencies all day every day. When my frequency runs across a similar song, my energy begins to vibrate with theirs, and a connection is made. Whether it be friendship or romance, there is an attraction when similar energies find one another. However, we also have most likely experienced a different feeling when we run across someone's energy that repels us. We might not know why, but some people just rub us the wrong way. Their signature frequency and ours are on different wavelengths and do not attract each other. We also see this principle at work with teams and organizations. If you get eleven men operating on similar frequencies in football, we call that momentum. When those same eleven start vibing in eleven different ways, we call that a slump.

Certain people have a higher frequency to their energy, and they become leaders. Their frequency is able to affect the collective energy of an entire group, and their team members begin to vibe like the leader. Whether it be a successful CEO or a powerful gang leader, the principle is the same. Collective energy becomes the culture of an organization and drives its success or failure. When we look at Gandhi, King, or Mandela, we see powerful frequencies that were able to move large numbers of people toward a common goal. Hitler also had a powerful frequency, and he almost took over the world.

So, if you take twelve hundred men who all have their own unique frequencies and put them in a closed space, over time that group will develop their own collective signature frequency. That will become the vibe, or the culture, of that prison. It is much like your favorite radio station, which comes in on a specific frequency, say 95.5. It can be country or jazz, rock or hip-hop, but that radio frequency always brings you similar music that makes you feel a certain way. If the prison's vibe is anger, fear, hate, and hopelessness, then everyone in that space gets caught up in that collective song, and they begin to flow that way.

We begin to talk about shifting the energy in their prison environment. If we can change one man's frequency at a time, then eventually we hit a tipping point and the signature frequency of the whole compound begins to change. We call it "changing the channel." Typically, I have found if we choose the right men, prison culture begins to shift when we have at least 10 percent of that prison's general population who have successfully completed the program. If we can change the frequency of the leaders, then we can change their followers soon after, and thus we can shift the energy of that prison toward positivity and true power.

The Five POPP Anchors

There is a series of questions I ask the brothers in every prison I go to. These questions bring all of them together and take away their excuses. These questions also win their respect, and maybe even some trust. These questions reveal things they all have in common and what they all desire. I call them POPP Anchors. Anchors hold a boat in place, so the wind and the waves don't blow it away, sink it, or shipwreck it. These brothers live in a storm and can't ever get away, so they need anchors more than most.

The first question is this: "How many of you want to do hard time?" No hands go up, no matter where the prison is or how hard the men are. They pride themselves on being able to do the hardest time imaginable, but deep down, no matter how bad you are, nobody *wants* to do hard time.

The second question: "How many of you want to go home today and never come back?" Every hand goes up, and I've never had anyone keep their hand down. No matter how long they've been there, nobody wants to stay, and everybody wants out as soon as possible.

The third question: "How many of you want your sons, little brothers, or grandsons to come here?" This one is sacred, and there is silence. Not one hand ever goes up. In those rooms there are so many broken, dysfunctional, angry, and wounded relationships between fathers and sons, but not one of them wishes this hell on their families. It goes against the natural order of things.

The fourth question: "How many of you know when something is about to happen before it pops off?" All the hands go up, as these men live in a place where you'd better have a finely tuned antenna that senses when things aren't quite right. Whether it's a vibe, a feeling, hair on the back of your neck, or quiet chatter, these brothers have heightened situational awareness.

And lastly, the fifth question: "How many of you believe you have the power collectively to stop most, if not all, of the violence on this compound if you have a good enough reason?" Once again, all the hands go up, as these brothers understand the power and influence they possess.

Then I recap: "Okay, none of you want to do hard time, all of you want to go home as soon as possible and never come back, none of you want your sons to follow you here, you know when violence is about to happen, and you have the power to stop if you want to. Correct?" They nod their heads in approval. And then the moment of truth: I say, respectfully, "If that is true, and you are men of your word, and you're still doing dirt and causing violence in this place, then you must be full of crap."

First, it's quiet. Then they begin to look at each other as if to say, "Did he really just say that to us?" Then they begin to laugh and admit that I'm right, and they respect the boldness and honesty. They shake their heads and say, "That dude is crazy, but we dig him!" Now I have their respect.

They say they are getting out and swear they're never coming back, and I believe in their hearts they really mean it. But there is a disconnect. Most of them think they are going to magically change when they get outside of the razor wire, but the truth is, every day we are practicing who we will be tomorrow. The truth is, wherever you go, there you are. If you're living like a convict inside, then you will be the exact same convict in the free world. If you keep doing what you've always done, then you'll keep getting what you always get. If you want to change your life, you must first change the way you think. The Five POPP Anchors are something we will revisit again and again throughout the process, as we have all agreed to be men of our word. In these places, their word is their bond, and they'll die for it. At least they say they will.

A Made Man

There is no way I could have the influence I have behind the wire without the right guys vouching for me. An essential part of the process lies in locating the most influential inmates, setting up introductions, and going to work to win their trust and respect. In the prison system, the importance of credibility and respect cannot be overstated. If I vouch for you, I am putting my reputation on the line, so prisoners are cautious about who they vouch for. I have been vouched for by one gang leader to another, as well as with powerful criminals on the streets. Then, for those who earn the right, I can vouch for them with prison officials, parole boards, and prospective employers in the free world, and that is one of the joys of my life. Somewhere along the way I became a "made man." To this day, they still insist I must have done time, because nobody could know as much about the chain gang as I do without having lived there. They thought the same about Johnny Cash, because he loved them so much and became their champion. They have made me one of their own. Once I am vouched for, then I can use my influence for positive change, and they allow me to.

I feel as though I owe it to them for changing my life. When I went inside for the very first time, something changed in me. I can't explain it, but a light came on and has been burning brighter and brighter ever since. They weren't who I thought they'd be. They were respectful for the most part and grateful for a connection to the free world. They had fascinating stories about their unique journeys, and I always found myself somewhere in their stories. They cared deeply about their families. They kept their word and did what they said they would do. Many had a desire to make a difference in the lives of kids after they got out, so the youth wouldn't make the same mistakes as they did. Many are faithful; many are brilliant artists; many are incredible writers and poets; some are tattoo artists and painters. I have the most beautiful etching of the Last Supper on the wall of my office, as well as other paintings my brothers behind the wire have given me. The etching was made for me by a death-row inmate in Alabama. My friend Michael was executed in 2019, after he asked for no more appeals to be made on his behalf. That picture reminds me of him every day.

The majority of the men who have gone through our Forty Days to Freedom program have willingly served when asked to help decrease the violence and work with administration to create a better quality of life for inmates and staff alike. They have earned the right for me to stand up for them. They are far from being unredeemable, and they are the only ones who can help turn the tide. If you get close enough to see who they really are, then you are much more likely to put your reputation on the line and try to open doors for them.

Now, with the respect they have given me and the influence they have allowed for me to have, my vouching for them in the free world is valuable to them, and something I do not take for granted. I also vouch for them with wardens and officers in their prisons, as I hopefully have earned their respect too. They have taught me how to connect with those who are hard to connect with—simply get the right people to vouch for you.

Honor among Thieves

It turns out there really is honor among thieves. I have witnessed a universal code in prisons around the world. The volunteer, or "Holy Man," as they often call us, is untouchable and off limits (though I am far from holy!). When people tell me to be careful in there, I typically respond by saying, "I'm safer in there than I am in the free world." There have been several threats along the way, but if anyone ever laid a hand on me, they would have real trouble. In the more dangerous prisons, I typically have a trusted bodyguard who has committed themselves to protecting me, though I've never asked for one nor do I desire one. They protect their own.

My most trusted friend behind the wire, Sir Brown, has been one of the most faithful brothers I've ever had. I know for a fact he has saved my life more than once in the early days when things got crazy in our first prison, before they knew what I was about. Once they learn I'm not trying to get guys out of their gangs or interrupt the flow of business, then they are cool with me; otherwise, I would be a threat. Interestingly, some of the most dangerous gang leaders are actually a significant part of our strategy for peace, as they have the most influence. Once they get on board, we have their whole gang behind us. I have found the code to be trustworthy, and some of the most dangerous men have the strongest word and often the most integrity. They say what they mean and mean what they say, and they rarely lie. They don't have to, so typically I can trust what they say. Is there really honor among prisoners? Often more so than in the free world.

Andre Broke the Code

The first name on our initial Forty Days of Peace pledge at our very first prison was Andre. Since then, thousands of inmates across the country and even south of the border have signed that same pledge, but Andre will always be the first. Andre was the first to publicly break the convict code and put himself at risk for POPP. Someone had to step out and practice the principles with an audience, and he was the brother who made that first move.

We were on day eleven in our very first Forty Days of Peace in the prison where the movement began. The brothers were journaling every day their victories, failures, epiphanies, and breakthroughs as they attempted to follow King, Gandhi, and Mandela. I didn't know it when I first met him, but Andre was just waiting for someone to call him to do something great. He was a high-ranking member of a national gang, and he had considerable influence. So, on day eleven, Andre was in his dorm playing cards with another inmate he didn't know very well. At one point in the game, the other inmate challenged Andre and accused him of cheating. Whenever something like this happens, the energy in the room shifts. Whether they hear it or not, people sense there's a situation. It was an open dorm, and suddenly all eyes were on Andre.

He sternly told the brother he had not cheated, and the rival cussed him and threatened him. As the other man stood, so did

The New Convict Code

Andre. Now everyone was watching. The next move in a confrontation is vital. You can lose a reputation in an instant and gain a new one as well, and it is all determined by the convict code. Andre had a new code he was about to test. The old code says you'd better swing fast and fight for respect, as you cannot let someone get away with a challenge like that in front of spectators. If you back down, then you are labeled a "free-pick," and the word gets out that you won't fight. But Andre had signed a pledge and committed to living nonviolently for forty days, and he is an honorable brother who keeps his word.

So, he reached out his hand and said, "Peace be with you, brother. I got nothing but love for you." The room was silent, and his rival was speechless. He reached down and slapped Andre's popcorn off the table and onto the floor. Andre calmly bent to his knees, cleaned up the popcorn, put it back on the table, and stood eye to eye with his opponent once again. He reached out his hand and said for the second time, "Peace be with you, brother." His adversary slapped his hand away, cussed him again, and walked out of the room. The witnesses muttered amongst themselves, wondering if Andre had gotten weak, because they knew he didn't handle himself that way.

The next day they were in the chow hall. Andre approached his adversary, and the man braced for conflict. For the third time, Andre extended the hand of peace and said, "All good, brother?" The man sat there and silently stared back with no reply. Andre simply said, "Peace," and walked away. Later that week, his rival came and found Andre in the dorm. He walked up to tell him everything was cool. He had heard about the brothers who had taken the peace pledge, as news was spreading around the camp.

Andre had prevailed without violence and had actually turned an enemy into a friend. The next week, another brother handled a conflict nonviolently on the basketball court, and another did the same in another dorm. The energy was changing, and the prisoners were watching. That was when more and more brothers began coming forward and inquiring about how they could join the peace movement. All they had to do was see the principles work with their own eyes, and they wanted in.

We are all built for peace, and nobody wants to do hard time. Sometimes it only takes one to turn the tide, and Andre was that one. We believed it would work, and now we knew it would—the convict code could be broken. Andre had earned a new kind of respect—one that lasts. He had a new code.

Chapter Seven
THE NEW POPP CODE

The convict code is broken and in desperate need of repair. It was developed over decades of men living in unlivable circumstances as a way to survive. While effective for those who run things, the code is dangerous and destructive because of the consequences for violations. However, the fact that two-million men are living by a standard code means we could have a major shift, rather quickly, if we can teach them a better way, a more effective code. They value their code, so we would start there. And that's exactly what we did.

The Power of Mantras

In our POPP program we have several important mantras that guide us. These are also anchors because they keep us grounded in the principles that will navigate us through the stormy waters. "Hope is the new dope" is an important one. Hope is a dangerous thing in a prison. For many of these prisoners, they gave up on hope a long time ago, and we challenge them to hope once again. I challenge them to risk a broken heart and long for their desires. Another mantra is "I am the power of peace." This mantra reminds them that in every interaction, they have the opportunity and responsibility to bring peace into the situation. This empowers them as a peacemaker and focuses them on solutions rather than problems. It reminds them they have true power within themselves.

One of the most important POPP mantras is "I see you, I feel you, I got you." They love this one. In this simple statement, we remind them of three crucial components on our journey to become peacemakers. "I see you" represents respect. It means they see their rival and recognize them for who they really are as men. They look past the skin color, the prison uniform, the tattoos, and their gang affiliations, and see the God inside of one another. This is a powerful anchor in their personal and collective development. Respect is a huge issue behind the wire. In one way or another, everything runs on respect. It's something you must earn. All eyes are on you all of the time, and judgments are formed in every interaction. Once you have gained respect, then you can do decent time. Sometimes you must fight somebody for it, and you can easily lose it if you're not careful. We teach the brothers that we begin with respect, before it is earned, and you see the man as you want them to be. If they lose your respect, then that is on them, but we will begin by respecting one another throughout the project. "I see you" is a powerful and effective mantra.

"I feel you" represents compassion. Compassion is rare in a prison, and a term you rarely hear. Compassion simply means you feel the pain of the other because you are both walking on the same path. It also means you feel the joy of the other and can celebrate victories with them. If I identify with your pain because I have experienced it myself, then I have the opportunity to move into empathy. If I don't feel your pain, then it's easy to hurt you. Empathy is missing in our society these days. Everyone judges, and few understand or relate to the other's pain. When I feel you, it's much harder to judge you or hate you.

"I got you" represents loyalty. Loyalty is another important

The New Convict Code

part of prison life. You must know who has your back and who you need to be careful with. If I say, "I got you," and then I'm not there for you when you need me, then I have real problems. Someone's loyalty must be earned. Once I develop some level of trust, then I might expect you to be there for me if I need you. I challenge the men to take a chance and commit to one another over the next forty days and be loyal to the program, loyal to the principles, and on some level, loyal to one another. They already know the importance of loyalty. Now, we expect them to practice it with others outside of their group, since we are on the same team.

"I see you, I feel you, I got you" is something we say a lot and continue to reinforce as we build our new team of prison peacemakers. If I treat you with respect, practice compassion with you, and commit my loyalty to you, then maybe we can begin to trust one another. Trust is such a rare and valuable commodity. For most of these men, all trust has been destroyed, and they have resigned themselves to never trust anyone or anything again. That's part of the convict code: Never trust anyone completely. We dare them to build trust again, which begins with trusting themselves. If we don't trust ourselves, then we will never trust one another.

The last POPP mantra we will discuss here is "I can do very hard things." This one is something my wife and I have used with our grandson. We can't remember where we first picked it up, but it helped him try to do things that scared him or that he felt were impossible. I use it with the inmates now and ask them to repeat it to themselves over and over until they believe it. I remind them they did some very hard things to get where they are, and I expect them to go after what they want now just as hard as they went after things in the free world. I remind them that they are the kind of men who are willing to do whatever it takes, and they have exhibited amazing courage at different times in their lives, even if it was misdirected. Let us begin with the courage and commitment they've had for various people and things in their lives, and apply that same energy to the hard things they are attempting now. An attitude of "I can do very hard things" reminds them what they are capable of and brings them together as a team.

The Influence of the POPP Wristband

In the beginning it was just a way to reward the brothers for their effort. A simple wristband was given to each participant at the beginning of each new POPP phase as a reminder of the pledge they had signed and the commitment they had made to one another and to themselves. But then the "I Am the Power of Peace" bands became so much more. Two brothers would be on the verge of an altercation, and a POPP leader would walk up and say, "Hey, brother, can't you see this man is on his Forty Days of Peace? Give him a break and pick this back up on day forty-one." The wristband could give a brother a way out without backing down, and this was significant. We began to simply say, "Day forty-one," when a brother was challenged, and that meant we would push pause and handle the conflict later, after the conclusion of the project. What we knew was that at the end of the forty days, they would most likely have forgotten the problem. It was so simple. They were moving the movement.

The wristbands became high in demand. They became a badge of courage. Every time a brother completed another phase, he got another wristband. The POPP veterans had as many as five bands, giving them a new kind of street cred. I even found out some brothers were selling them for ten dollars apiece, but we had to put an end to that. You had to earn them; you couldn't simply buy them. On one occasion, one of my favorite wardens told me a shank had been confiscated and it had one of our wristbands wrapped around the handle for a grip. I was so disappointed. Then she said, "No, don't worry. An officer did it." I was relieved, but also disheartened to see how some of the officers felt about these men getting some peace in their lives. I've had a harder time bringing the correctional officers together than these hardened convicts. It's a sad state of affairs, but we'll keep working until we get them too.

Rules vs. Agreements

The current system is built on rules and lockdowns. Break the rules, and you'll get locked down. Break them enough, and you will catch more time. Break the wrong rules, and you might never get out. Certainly, I understand we must have the rule of law, and there must be consequences for actions. However, if there is no incentive or reward built into the system, it breaks a man's spirit. Add to it that they are living in an environment where men who are doing long bids, with little to no hope, are running things, and you have more violence. When you add the missing ingredient of hope, things begin to change.

These men once had hope, even if it was very little, depending on where and by whom they were raised. Broken promises and burnt bridges are the norm. Families often stop visiting, and the letters stop coming. The money is no longer put on the books, and they no longer have store call, which makes them feel less than human. Oftentimes the officers treat them like they are worthless, and eventually they believe it. When we arrive, we seek to give them something more powerful than money, drugs, or food. They are dared to hope and challenged to dream, even if it's for the first time.

They have assimilated into a world of rules, rules they never really chose or agreed to. That doesn't change the fact they must obey the rules or face the consequences. On one side, they have the rules of the convict code with serious consequences for violations. But on the other side, they have the administration rules that have been set by the system they have been sentenced into. So, which do you obey? Sometimes they conflict, so you have a decision to make: Obey the warden or obey the code. You can guess who wins, and that pits the men in white against the men in black once again, and gives the authorities yet another reason to lock 'em down.

We are obligated to obey rules, and if you do not wish to, then you either have to be very good at concealing violations or else face the consequences when you get caught. Agreements, on the other hand, are different. We offer the men a third option, which the authorities as of yet do not: an agreement between two parties. An agreement, according to *Merriam-Webster*, is "an arrangement as to a course of action." This means they are a part of the transaction and they've helped to construct the agreed-upon arrangement. There is power in agreement because you have a meeting of the minds between the two parties. Parents should consider this with teenagers. Of course, there are going to be strict rules that aren't negotiable, but there are many areas where kids can be a part of constructing the plan and establishing healthy accountability.

These men who live behind the wire are much more honorable than the masses think. Of course they want less violence; of course they want more humane living conditions; of course they want more privileges and freedoms; of course they want a better quality of life. It just makes sense to me to involve them in the process, so that is what we have done in several prisons across the country, and it works. I ask them what they truly want, and we come up with a constructive plan to bring about their realistic demands. But here is the rub: They must give me something to work with when I fight for them with the administration. I have to have something to bargain with, and some leverage. The most obvious place to begin is the violence. Until violence is reduced, all bets are off. If they keep living violently, attacking each other and the staff, then the authorities will be justified to continue meeting force with force, violence with violence, and darkness with darkness. And the cycle repeats.

So, I dare them to be a part of the solution, rather than the problem. This empowers them and makes them feel like men again. They now feel important and powerful. They are rising to the level of how we see them once again. At one prison there was no hot water in one of the dorms, and the dorm happened to be the most violent on the compound simply because they had so many rival gangs housed together. The authorities were more than happy to let them continue taking cold showers because of the violence. So, I asked the warden if I could go back there whenever I was at the prison for my weekly POPP meeting, and she agreed. However, they had no idea why anyone would want to hang out in such a dangerous dorm if they didn't have to. I asked a few of the more powerful guys who lived in that dorm if it was cool for me to come by and visit occasionally. Of course they agreed, because I am their connection to the free world. Next, I asked the brother who had the most influence in that dorm what I could do for them that would help their living conditions. I knew the answer before it was given: Fix the showers.

He and I began to have weekly conversations, and we became friends. He happened to be a Blood leader. I asked him what it would take to cut down the violence in his dorm, and he said that was easy, just say the word. They had a spot behind the showers that they called the Horseshoe. This was where fights typically happened because there were no cameras in that area. I asked if we could have meetings there, and he was impressed that I already knew about the Shoe. Around there, that was street cred. This gave me influence with both the inmates and the staff. He told me if I didn't want violence, he would see to it, and I told him I would see about those showers. It didn't take long, and the solution was quite simple. However, it couldn't have happened without the brothers in white being in agreement. See how easy this is? They hate the rules, but they love solutions, especially if both parties agree.

Fear vs. Love

There is compassion hiding inside of dangerous prisons in America. I bet you've never heard that before. Kindness in a prison? How about we take it even further: kindness among rival gangs in maximum-security prisons. Let's go further still: kindness among gang members in juvenile prisons. Kindness is becoming more and more rare in today's stressed-out, cynical world. People have become fear-based and defensive. Many won't even look you in the eye anymore. And now with the pandemic, people are masked up, socially distanced, and unable to hug. This makes the problem even worse.

There are only two fundamental perspectives through which we see the world: through a lens of love or a lens of fear, and the two are mutually exclusive. When fear is dominant, we are not acting out of love. This doesn't mean we're not going to be afraid, but it does mean perfect love overcomes fear and drives it out. If we live in fear long enough, it becomes our setpoint emotionally and mentally. Worrying, fretting, and seeking more drama becomes the norm, and we can even get addicted to it. Kindness is the casualty when we are on the run or fighting against life. Albert Einstein said, "The most important decision we make is whether we believe we live in a friendly or hostile universe." Love or fear, and which one you choose, makes all the difference.

We are seeing the effects of fear in our culture today as more and more people are literally getting hooked on drama. Stress, worry, and panic cause the body to overproduce adrenaline, as we are in a constant state of fight-or-flight. However, the vast majority of the time, our worst fears never come to pass, and we have simply created psychological fear. There is no one to fight and nothing to run from, but the brain doesn't care when it is stuck in a looping cycle of anxiety. It shifts into survival mode, and it doesn't make good decisions in a state of fight-or-flight. On top of all that, stress can play a significant role in heart disease, cancer, accidental death, suicide, overdose, and violence. So the question is, have you become addicted to drama with all that is going on in our crazy world? The brain gets hooked on whatever it does the most, and that is bad news for many these days.

When someone comes from a place of love rather than fear, we see amazing things. We see courage and authenticity, sacrifice and service, humility and integrity, loyalty and perseverance. When we remain in a state of fear, we see rage and anger, depression and anxiety, defensiveness and divisiveness. The latter are what we are witnessing on the streets, in Congress, and even in our own households.

Now imagine living inside a maximum-security prison. The whole system works off of fear. Whether you are staff or resident, fear is an everyday way of life. You're either causing fear, or you're living in fear being surrounded by predators. You never know when a guy is about to snap. Sir Brown told me one time that you have to be careful with every man in there. A weak and cowardly man might be on his last thread, and this is the day he says, "No more. The next one to come at me is going to die, or they're going to have to kill me." The officers never know when it could be their day too.

So, why in the world would we expect to find kindness and compassion in a prison? Because they're hungrier for it than we are, they're willing to go to greater lengths to attain it, and more of them want it than the ones who don't. Men give in to an angry, fear-based life when they believe there are no other options. However, when they find a better way, and begin to see even the gang leaders striving to practice acceptance, it gives them hope and they try. Once they get a little bit of kindness and compassion in such a dark place, they crave it, and they get hooked on it. Hope really is the new dope.

A program I have partnered with in Atlanta is called Canine CellMates. Inmates are partnered with rescued dogs who have been abused and neglected. They form a special bond in their pain. Both are in need of healing, and they learn to help one another. The power of the program is in the kindness and compassion they show one another. They both learn to trust after they've been hurt and abused, and the outcome is transformative. Once they have allowed themselves to be loved unconditionally and do the same for their canine partner, then, just maybe, they can do the same in their human relationships. I've even worked in a prison in Kentucky that utilizes this program, but instead of dogs, they use horses. You can imagine how popular this program is with the brothers behind the wire.

Canine CellMates in Atlanta

Ego Force vs. Soul Force

Today we see a nation trapped in ego. In many ways I believe we are reaping what we have sown. I was born in 1964 and still remember black-and-white TV with rabbit ears, and I can still recall how excited we were when eight-track tapes first came out in the seventies. Today we are planning to colonize Mars in the not-too-distant future, and artificial intelligence is becoming a reality. Technology has created a world where everything is at our fingertips. Faster, easier, and more comfortable and convenient is how we expect it, and we lose our minds when we don't get it. No need to go to the store anymore; we'll just bring it to you with instant delivery services. We've allowed screens to raise our kids; we've glorified sex, as well as murder, rape, and mayhem in our movies, music, and video games. We have made being rich and famous the ultimate goal, and we've cared little for the marginalized and the least of these. What we glorify, we eventually become, and here we are. Ego has run amok, and we are reaping the whirlwind.

The ego is the false self, a construct of the mind. It begins when we are young as we become aware of me, mine, you, and yours, and establish boundaries. However, as we grow, it can run wild and cause all kinds of problems—for ourselves as well as others. The ego is the illusionary self that we have unconsciously created based on who we believe ourselves to be. It is defined by our reputation, profession, race, religion, education, geography, gender, title, and the list goes on and on. Often it is grounded in talent, physique, skin tone, perceived beauty, strength, popularity, wealth, athleticism, and social status. When I attach to labels, and define myself and others by worldly standards, I am separating myself from who I truly am. What happens if and when we lose those things? We face a crippling identity crisis.

The world would describe me as a white male, tall and thin, upper-middle class, Southern, athletic, Christian, educated, married, self-employed, and entrepreneur. Does that sum me up? Is that all that I am? What if I gained weight, moved north, got divorced, left my religion, and went to work for someone else? Would that change who I really am? Labels do not define me, and that's why I refuse to wear them. As it has been said, "When you label me, you negate me." The ego is easily offended, always defending, sneaky, and insecure. It lashes out, throws fits, seeks revenge, plots, and schemes. The ego is terrified of annihilation, likes to hide, but also needs the spotlight. It is arrogant and selfish, and has a hard time working with others. It compares, criticizes, mopes, and feels sorry for itself. The ego is never satisfied and always longs for more. Never peaceful in the present moment, the ego always tries to get out of right here and right now so it can get on to the next thing. It becomes obsessed with the past, worried about the future, and lives in regret, fear, and isolation. Kind of sounds like the world we are living in, doesn't it?

The soul, on the other hand, is pure God stuff. The word "soul" comes from the same Greek word as "self," *psychi*. Psychology is the study of self. It is the golden ball of light that came into the world wrapped in flesh. It is the eternal self that will return back to its source one day. It is pure and made of one substance, and it is timeless and always content. It has no need to defend, it is not easily angered, and it never gets offended. The soul knows where it came from, why it's here, and where it is going. It is secure and confident, it lives in love and not fear, and it never seeks revenge or even desires it; it does not hoard or withhold, but freely gives. It does not live in scarcity, but plenty. It does not even fear death, as it is not bound by the human body, and death is merely a beautiful release.

Now I want for you to imagine a hundred tough, hard, stubborn prisoners sitting spellbound and listening to the things I just wrote, but hearing it live and with passion. Slowly they come alive, and their countenance changes. The hard exterior softens and their heart sheds a few more layers of pain. Prisons are pure ego, and when the dam breaks and they let light in, they are desperate for more. I'm telling you, trust me now, believe me later: Prisons are a ripe and fertile field for light and soul liberation.

The POPP Brothers at Marion

Bama and the Heartless Felons

One of my favorite prisons is in Marion, Ohio, and one of my favorite wardens is the man who was in charge during the years I facilitated POPP there. Jason Bunting is creative, proactive, and progressive in regard to prison reform. In my experience, that is rare. For that, he gets my utmost respect, and he turned out to be a big part of the early development of the Power of Peace Project. When the warden and staff at a prison get behind the program and support it, it goes extremely well. It must be a partnership if the change is going to be sustainable.

Much of the success of the POPP movement in Marion is due to Jason's personal involvement and the intentional way he selected the participants. One example is a man they call "Bama." Bama has been incarcerated for thirty-five years and had been leading the Aryan Brotherhood gang for a long time at this prison. The Aryans are white supremacists and are very dangerous. In many prisons they specialize in contracts, meaning if you want to kill an inmate, the Aryan Brotherhood will carry it out for a fee. The warden knew we would need Bama's influence, so he invited him personally. Bama declined because he didn't do programs. Most of the guys you need to shift the culture in a prison are not your typical program inmates. So, Jason asked again and said, "Just come to the first night for me. If you don't like it, then you don't have to come back." Bama agreed with some hesitation.

I didn't meet this man on the first night, but I saw him. Large and heavyset, Bama has long hair, a long beard, and Coke-bottle glasses. He has a big scar on his nose where someone tried to bite it off. On that first night, Bama just watched and took it all in. To the warden's surprise, he showed up for the second session the next morning. He kept to himself for the most part, but he was

The New Convict Code

assigned to sit at a table with a group of young black inmates who were part of a gang called the Heartless Felons. They're an aggressive gang that formed in the juvenile system, and now they're causing serious problems as they are bound over into adult prisons. They recruit heavily and will coerce young inmates through violence or extortion until they join. The head of the Heartless Felons was seated at Bama's table.

However, things went fairly smoothly in the beginning as everyone took the forty-day peace pledge. Each week, the groups met together at their assigned tables and began to go through the curriculum and the discussions that followed. It's an amazing thing to witness. When rivals get close enough together, for a long enough period of time, with intentional conversation, hatred and judgment fall away. Hatred and judgment happen at a distance, but understanding and reconciliation happen up close and personal.

Everyone was quite surprised when Bama was chosen by his table to speak at the graduation celebration. This is quite an honor because your paper has to get chosen and you must have shown some leadership throughout the forty days. The fact that his group chose him to represent them was a big deal. Every participant must write a paper on their "Champion of Peace." They can choose one of the peacemakers featured in the book, or they can choose someone who had a lasting positive impact on their life. They cannot receive their POPP Certificate of Achievement without turning in a paper.

When Bama got up to present his paper, the chapel grew quiet. As he began, his eyes began to well up. He cleared his throat and said, "Sorry, I've got heartburn," and everyone laughed. Before he began to read, he said, "Eight weeks ago, I wouldn't even sit with them," and he pointed over to his table filled with young black guys. He continued, "But today, after everything we've gone through together, those brothers are my family. I still might not share a cell with them, but I don't hate 'em anymore." Everyone broke into applause. I want you to understand what an amazing thing that was—please don't miss it. An Aryan Brotherhood white-supremacist gang leader standing in front of his peers and rivals, and publicly embracing his former enemies. He was putting his life in danger.

Afterward, he was so proud of himself, but not in a boastful way. He had done something significant and completed something he could forever be proud of. He spoke of the way it made him feel when he rode his Harley through the mountains on a sunny day back in the free world. He compared this feeling to that one. Self-esteem is like that, and many of these men have never accomplished anything of this value or significance. Maybe he would send his certificate home to his family, or maybe he would hang it in his cell. I wondered how his Nazi brothers would feel about it.

When I returned for my next visit, Bama was there. He came up and gave me a big bear hug, and then I noticed something was different about him. I couldn't put my finger on it, so I asked. He said, "It's my glasses. I don't have them anymore."

I said, "What happened, did you get contacts?" Which was a dumb question; they don't get contacts behind the wire.

He replied, "No, somebody came into my cell and stomped them out."

I thought to myself that no one would have dared do that a few months ago. I said, "Wow, you let somebody get away with that?" You see, I don't teach them to be weak, but rather to develop strength under control. Then he told me what happened. A guard came into his cell and shook it down, then he took his glasses and smashed them with his boot. I told him how sorry I was, and that I was proud of his self-control.

It's sad, but one of the biggest challenges we encounter with POPP comes not from the inmates, but the correctional officers. Many of them don't want the brothers to be happy or to grow and change, so they "try" them and attempt to get them to lose their peace. If they can get a brother to retaliate, then they can send him to the hole, which discredits the program. But Bama didn't retaliate, which is quite something. After that episode, I began asking wardens for an opportunity to make a presentation to the security staff before we launched, so that they would at least know what the prisoners were attempting. I ask them to encourage the little changes they see, especially from the knuckleheads, or at least not make it harder for the brothers who are really trying to change.

At the Marion POPP celebration, we had good news to announce. Over those last two months during the project there was only one act of violence among the participants, a 99 percent success rate. The one brother who did get into an altercation was defending himself and did not initiate it. However, we don't have asterisks. I am so proud of these men; all they needed was a big *why* and the tools to achieve success. I believe this model can work anywhere with anybody, as long as they make an honest effort.

Chapter Eight
PUNISHMENT VS. REWARD

POPP Graduation Celebration at La Mesa Prison in Tijuana

The current correctional system works for those in charge but has no realistic chance of rehabilitating offenders. Punitive justice with no incentive or reward discourages and disheartens prisoners and turns many of them toward a violent lifestyle. Most of them are returning someday, but just who will they be when they revisit our communities? Most are coming home racist and angry, ready to live how they've been practicing on the inside. I often tell them the way they are living behind the wire is exactly the way they will live when they get out, because we are practicing today who we will be tomorrow.

Punitive justice works in the short term to control the inmate population, but it rarely changes behavior long term. If you only punish a kid for wrongdoing, and never reward him, then you will raise an insecure and bitter child. They will rebel or hide, depending on their nature. Either way, they don't really learn the lessons of reward for the right behavior, but instead become sophisticated liars who are experts at not getting caught. That is how the current correctional system operates, and it's no wonder the recidivism rate is so high. Recidivism is the percentage of inmates who reoffend and go back to prison within the first three years of their release. However, if they learn to do right in order to receive good things while in prison, they are preparing to build a life in the free world based on reward for good behavior and hard work, rather than being locked down every time they make a bad choice. Which is more powerful and effective: hope of reward, or fear of punishment?

This broken system can be changed, but only if both sides want it. So far, I've seen dangerous men choose to do the hard thing, but I haven't seen the other side be as willing to make serious changes. Not yet. I believe they will, but only when the public has seen enough to demand true reform. Punitive justice is predictable; incentive-based corrections is unpredictable. Punishment is measurable, while reward-based programs are more invisible, because it is harder to measure things that never happen. You wouldn't believe all the dangerous drama the brothers behind the wire have prevented. I've seen beautiful things that prison administrators were never even aware of. These men want peace, and they want to be treated as men. That's all any of us want.

Three Punishments for One Crime

When a person is charged, convicted, and sentenced for certain crimes, the next stop is typically a state prison. If the sentence is shorter, sometimes they will do their time in a county jail. Being separated from the life you have built is tough punishment, as you are removed from your family and friends, your job or career, your school or trade, your church and social life, and whatever else you might possess. You are disconnected from society altogether, and you lose all your ties to the free world. You give up all of your possessions, your choices, your hobbies, your routines, and often your future. That is what prison was intended to be: your removal from society, for a time, to protect the community. That alone is severe punishment, as you lose all you cherish and hold dear.

However, in this country you are punished a second time by having to live in a place where the food is practically inedible, there is rarely air conditioning, and the heat can rise to over one hundred degrees in your cell. There is little to no health, dental, or mental health care. You are harassed at every turn, you are confined to your tiny cell the majority of the time, and gangs run the facilities. You are forced to work a job with little to no pay, you have to watch your back night and day, and the list goes on and on.

Then you are punished yet a third time upon your release. A felony follows you on every application for employment, housing, or education, which makes it extremely tough to start over again. By the time a brother or sister is let out, they have been stripped of most of their basic human rights, and it is very difficult to regain them. These forfeited rights include, depending on the state, voting, jury duty, international travel, employment in certain professions, parental rights, public assistance and housing, purchasing and possessing a firearm, and more. It is not surprising that two-thirds return to the streets and reoffend, or get revoked and go back inside.

Then they must satisfy the parole and probation system, which is also difficult. You can be revoked and sent back if you are in the presence of a firearm or another convicted felon; if you test dirty on a drug screen; if you fail to report to your meeting with your parole officer; if you catch another charge, even a misdemeanor;

or if you fail to pay your monthly fees. We have stacked the deck against former inmates, and made it hard, if not impossible, to assimilate back into the free world and build a decent life. Many choose to go back to the only life they have ever known, on the streets, only to repeat the cycle and eventually go back into the system as a repeat customer.

It is true—many rise above and find a way, which is admirable—but most have never seen success on the outside and cannot even imagine it for themselves. Parole and probation violations are an easy way to send them back to the life they have learned behind the wire. Punishment is only effective if the goal is to keep them as wards of the state to continue producing the goods we take for granted every day. However, there is a better way.

County Jails and the NFL

As our prison peace initiative became more and more effective, I began being invited to county jails as well. Jails are much different from prisons. In a prison, men have already been charged, convicted, and sentenced, and are doing time in the facility where they will be for a while. While still violent and dangerous, prisons are more predictable and stable because the inmates live there and know their fate, rather than staying in county for a relatively short time and waiting to find out what is next.

However, in a jail most of the men have only been charged, but not convicted or sentenced yet. Some are there for misdemeanors and will stay only a couple of months, and many are there for felonies but still waiting for a trial date, which can take months or even years. So jails are less predictable and are more unstable, as the players are constantly changing, guys often know each other from the streets and bring their beefs inside, and there is extra tension that comes from not knowing the outcome of their case and not knowing where they're going or how long they will be there. So, with such a high turnover rate, it's hard to find the right influencers and have the time to develop the momentum we need for our campaign to be a success.

In the particular jail I was invited to, they were experiencing escalating violence in their highest-security block. This wasn't the first rodeo for most of these men, as many had done real time before they caught their latest case. This jail is rather large, as far as jails go, with about two thousand residents. When I received the invitation, I was excited for a new challenge. I do believe there is a place for POPP in jails; we just needed to make a few adjustments to account for the differences from regular prison life.

The key is incentive, so I just needed to find out what was important to these men. First of all, in county jails the sheriff requires that the men be in cuffs and shackles when working with volunteers. So, my first move was to see how quickly those could be removed so the brothers would feel more like free men. I was told that if the men did well for the first two weeks, we could remove the restraints. The men did really well, so they were removed, as promised. You have no idea what that little move meant to them. One brother told me that was what earned his respect, because I did what I told them I would, which he said was rare. Secondly, we told them we would bring in pizza and soda if they continued their good work, and again they were rewarded. You would not believe how grateful these brothers are for things I take for granted every day. But we needed a big win for them to strive for—and we found it with NFL football.

With the current correctional model, privileges and freedoms are taken away for violations, but rarely, if ever, are things given to them for positive behavior. So, with the uptick in violence in the block we were working in, their beloved football had been taken away. That by itself can cause even more violence. Sports are something they cherish because it takes them away, if only for a minute, from the hell they live in and reminds them of the free world. They are angry when things get taken away, and often there is retribution for those who caused it. But what if positive changes happen? What if the ones who brought about that change were rewarded? They would be more highly respected by the brothers who shared in that reward.

That was our carrot. If they did well for the next two weeks, then they would get their Sunday football back. They were motivated and continued their good work. You should have seen their gratitude when football returned, and we made sure all the other brothers on the block knew who to thank for this special gift. How can you hate a guy when he is responsible for making your life better? But here is the real power behind this part of the program: When conflicts were escalating between brothers on the block, a POPP guy would come up and say, "You better work this thing out, brothers. Don't you dare get our football taken away again." Do you see that? Now they were policing themselves to protect the freedom they had earned, and that is exactly what happens on a larger scale in our prison program. They protect what is valuable to them, and then they get hooked on a better quality of life. So, when new guys come in, they quickly find out what the expectations are and that they had better not rock the boat. That is a brand-new convict code, one that is founded on reward rather than punishment, which is much more powerful and sustainable. We even had a former NFL player at their graduation celebration.

In one of our prisons the warden let one of our POPP leaders speak to the guys right after they got off the bus and arrived at intake. They were informed there was a peace initiative at their prison and to ask around if they wanted in. Imagine the relief a guy must feel as he's led into a dangerous prison for the first time. They are immediately interested in how they can become involved.

In Michigan, the movement was rolling, and a brother came along who began to threaten a good thing. He was pretending to be a POPP leader, but behind the scenes he was robbing and extorting and threatening our good reputation with administration. The Peace Council got together, and one brother actually proposed he be dealt with. Cooler heads prevailed, and he was told to trust God. The following week, the brother who was causing trouble was magically shipped out to another prison. They had learned another powerful lesson: Keep planting good seeds and trust the Universe to work on your behalf. We've never had any of our POPP brothers take matters into their own hands to straighten out a hypocrite, and that's why we construct peace councils that work hand in hand with the wardens and staff.

POPP Brothers and the NFL

Too Tired to Fight

If I could make only a few changes to decrease violence and bring about a significant shift in today's prison culture, one change I would make would be to add more recreation and competitive sports leagues. When violence rises, programs, sports, and recreation are taken away, and often never returned. When men are locked down and bored, they get into trouble, both on the chain gang and in the free world. When men get restless and have no outlet for their energy, they will find ways to "work out," even if that means violence. When men get to run and compete, and wear themselves out, then they have much less energy to fight at night. It also awakens their competitive spirit, which leads to new outlets and new ways to release frustrations and pent-up anger. It's going to come out somehow, so why not let them work things out on the court or field?

Typically, the brothers who are running things behind the wire tend to be stronger, more talented, and more athletic than the next guy, just like in the free world. If they have a way to compete on the field or the court, then a lot of aggression is released in a positive way. If we reward them when they win, and give them special recognition, then they will protect their sports and be motivated not to lose them. Hence, they will begin to police themselves, which only helps administration. As violent assaults on inmates and staff decline, we can simply reward them with more privileges. I would even consider bringing back boxing, but only with head gear. Men need an outlet for their pent-up energy and aggression.

Some will counter that if we get these guys out on the field, they will not be able to handle the temptation to get at one of their enemies. First of all, they are already doing that in the dorms and in the chow hall. Secondly, I have seen the opposite every time. At a maximum-security prison in Georgia where we operate, they have leagues, championships, and trophies, and they even have a Super Bowl. This last season the most violent dorm on the compound won the Super Bowl, and we rewarded them with a POPP trophy modeled after the NFL Vince Lombardi Trophy. You should have seen their pride and joy. They had their dorm name engraved on it and displayed in the trophy case. The last thing they want to do is screw up their chance to win again and repeat as champions. The participants, while sometimes violent, behaved as well as or better than the players you see on TV. The inmates are also the referees, and it is so inspiring to see them submit to one another out of love for the game. Reward is so much more powerful than punishment.

Wages for Labor

As of 2020 there are three states remaining that do not pay inmates anything for their labor. And the ones that do, pay an average of about twenty-five to fifty cents an hour—just a few dollars a day. Some states pay as little as ten cents an hour, and my state, Georgia, doesn't pay a thing. That is hard for me to get my head around. The inmates make different goods, depending on which state prison they reside in and which industries that state facility is contracted with. Some inmates make optical glasses, some make mattresses, others make clothing, while some make Kevlar vests. Even Victoria's Secret products were produced by inmates until that fact became public and they discontinued. These goods are sold in the free world for healthy profit to the states, while the brothers behind the wire work hard and are compensated little to nothing for their labor.

Imagine being assigned a detail, and you are penalized if you choose not to work. When a prisoner has no money on his books, whether it be because he has no family or his family has let him go, he must borrow or hustle. Neither of these is a good option, because when you owe on the inside, failure to pay can have dire consequences. When you hustle, you might cut in on someone else's livelihood, which has another set of potential consequences. If a man has a little money in his prison account, he can at least have store call and buy something, even if it's soup, some coffee, or hygiene goods, and it makes him feel a little more like a man. If he has nothing, he has little to look forward to, and he remains hungry and angry. Would you work a full day for little to no pay? Or, would you choose not to go and simply face the consequences? This is a broken system built to fail. It takes away a man's dignity and strips him of his pride. Then we wonder why many live like animals.

When a brother who has money on his books goes to commissary and buys his necessities or his favorite treats, he must walk back across the yard with his nylon sack over his shoulder. All eyes are on him, especially if he is new around there. Now the powerful force of envy begins to operate. Envy is often overlooked as one of the deadliest sins. In prison, it drives much of the darkness. "If I can't have it, then I don't want you to have it." Now imagine you're a lifetime criminal and you are thoroughly acquainted with the game. Your whole life is a hustle, and you have mastered the convict code. An easy and obvious hustle is to get to that newbie first and extort him. Often, they will set up a robbery and then offer to provide protection—for a fee. On each following Thursday, when that new brother comes back from store call, he must give a portion to his protector. So, even if you have money coming in from family or friends in the free world, that money is not necessarily yours. Many choose not to have it at all, because no one can hide that sack on the long walk back to the dorm, and hungry eyes are always watching.

Some naïvely say, "Just keep your head down and mind your business, and everything will be okay." While well-intentioned, what they fail to understand is that behind the wire you can't mind your own business because your business is everybody's business. The whole game runs on information, and information travels fast. Twelve hundred men in close proximity, with everyone on high alert at all times, makes for an interesting communication system. You rarely, if ever, have significant time alone, and you are most likely being videoed throughout the day everywhere you go. It is dangerous to trust anyone, because everyone is out to do the easiest time possible, and anyone can turn on you at any time.

So, you basically have three options: Join a gang for protection, give in to extortion and become what they call a "free pick," or fight long enough until they get the message that you won't give up or give in. When you get transferred to another camp, which can be frequently, you have to build your reputation all over again. And if you do affiliate for protection and then get transferred to another facility, you can't back out because word will get to where you're headed before you do. The bottom line is that if you have no way to make a little honest money, then you have to play among the wolves.

If we paid inmates for their labor, then we would be preparing them to earn an honest living when they return to the free world. They would also be less likely to be involved in criminal behavior while inside and would develop much-needed self-esteem, which would serve them when they are released. It would also help to alleviate much of the bitterness that develops toward administration and staff because of forced labor with no compensation.

Credit for Good Time

Some states have what is called "good-time credit." It is the time given back to inmates as a reward for following prison rules and staying out of trouble during their sentence. Good-time credit reduces a prisoner's time in prison. This is an obvious solution to what ails the prison system at large. If a man or a woman has a good enough reason to avoid trouble and follow the rules, then typically they will make better choices. If they are tempted to break a rule and they know they might get punished if they do, then it depends on the severity of the punishment as to whether they obey. Many of these men have gotten so hard and bitter over years of abuse, they just say, "Bump the rules, I'll take my chances and try not to get caught." But if someone gives you something to strive for, something you really want, if you simply do things right, then chances are, when you are presented with an opportunity to lie, cheat, or steal, then perhaps you will make a better choice. That is a much more powerful motivation.

That's how things work in the free world: Work hard and you'll get a raise, stay faithful and you'll keep a wife, save money and you can buy a house, tell the truth and you will be trusted. Incentive is so much more powerful than punishment. So, why would we not make good time credit a standard practice in corrections? Pay a man a reasonable wage for his labor and give him incentive to get out earlier if he flies straight. Freedom is what they want more than anything, so why not let them earn it? Or, we can just keep locking them down when they break the rules, pay them nothing for their work, and keep threatening more time if they keep disobeying. Which one do you think has a better chance of solving the mountain of problems we have created in the prison system in America? If you worked for free, were penalized if you didn't report as ordered, and could never leave that job or ever advance, would you continue working with a great attitude? Or, would you look for ways to improve your position, even if it meant breaking the rules? We are daring them to hustle, and then piling on the penalties when they do.

Hope for Young Offenders

I've spent the majority of my time over the years working on the intervention side of prison reform, striving to interrupt and redirect leaders in tough prisons to change their ways and be change agents to bring about a better quality of life for fellow residents. However, the pandemic put a swift halt to that work, as prisons and jails stopped allowing volunteers and non-employees into their facilities to protect inmates and staff. This was quite a challenge, as momentum is everything when trying to change a prison's culture. So, I had to focus on finding new and creative programs to bring about prison reform. There are two areas that are crucial to repairing this broken system: prevention and re-entry. Doors began to open, until the prisons were closed to free-world trainers and teachers because of COVID.

First, we'll look at prevention. I have done quite a bit of work in schools trying to keep kids in class, off the streets, off drugs, and out of gangs so they can pursue their dreams. I have sought to find effective programs to shatter the pipeline from schools to prisons for the kids who are already being attracted to the streets. Unfortunately, I have not come across many such programs. I've also been interested in effective re-entry programs that aim to dismantle the revolving door of repeat offenders and those being revoked into the system for probation and parole violations. In many ways the current probation and parole system is a money racket, and those in charge are reaping the rewards.

As you've heard before, "When one door closes, another opens," and that is exactly what happened for me during the quarantine. I was invited by Judge Wayne Grannis, the juvenile-court judge in Cobb County, Georgia, to join a pilot program called RISING designed to give youth offenders a second chance and an alternative to incarceration. This is his baby, and he has assembled an incredible team. Probation Supervisor of Gang Suppression Sharon Mashburn has been a valuable partner and has a huge heart for at-risk youth. It is a one-of-a-kind program built along the same lines as drug-and-alcohol accountability courts. The kids range from ages fourteen to seventeen and have already been charged, convicted, and sentenced for crimes that appear to be gang-related. They're on their way to jail. If chosen for this program, these young people enter a twelve-month intensive accountability court where they appear before the judge weekly and are accountable for their grades, drug screens, counseling, and other various assignments mandated by the court.

The judge has built a team of professionals around them: a gang specialist, a defense attorney, a family therapist, a probation officer, a guardian *ad litem*, a life coach, a mental health counselor, and others. If they are instructed to stay away from certain individuals, and they are caught not doing so, then the judge might order an ankle bracelet and thirty-day house arrest. The same could be the case for a dirty drug screen or missing scheduled appointments. It is so inspiring to watch these young people's progress and see them rise to the challenges they are given. When the participants successfully complete the six phases over the twelve-month period, their records are expunged, and *all* their charges go away. This program is one that could be replicated across the country, and thousands of young people could get the help they need before they go into the system, get a state number, and become yet another product in this repeat-customer business model.

Hope for Returning Citizens

Now let's look at re-entry. Another program I was tapped for is a pilot that helps returning citizens get back on their feet as they come out of prisons and jails. As already discussed, in our nation approximately two-thirds of the men and women who are released from prison or jail reoffend or get revoked within three years of their release. This is a dreadful and unacceptable success rate. There are a number of reasons for this alarming statistic. One, many of them cannot or should not go back to where they came from, as that is the environment that got them into trouble in the first place. Because of this, many of them have no place to stay. Two, felons have a hard time finding a job with a felony on their record, especially in the current job market. Many go back to hustling on the streets only to reoffend and go back into the system. Three, they have no real structure or discipline and no mentor or healthy accountability to help them do what many of them have never done before. Four, many are coming out with substance abuse issues and have no connection to support groups or recovery programs. And five, many of those coming out haven't completed a high school education, so a trade school or educational path is a real challenge for them to even comprehend.

There is a solution. Tip Top Poultry is a company in my hometown of Marietta, Georgia, that has been in business for over sixty years. This is a faith-based company, and the owner and his executive staff have a heart for returning citizens based on Jesus' teaching regarding how we treat the "least of these." They reached out to me when they were constructing their model because they wanted a motivational and inspirational piece to help participants through the tough times they will invariably go through when they are tempted to go back to the streets for easy money. Working at a poultry plant is very hard work for not a lot of pay, and turnover and retention rates are big issues in that industry. Low barriers to entry provide lots of applicants, but many have never held a job long-term or worked so hard, and they end up quitting. This company wanted to help those coming out of prison, but they also needed help retaining the workers they employed.

We set up a time to go to the local jail and address the inmates who were getting ready to go home, typically within three to six months of release, some shorter. We also pulled from transition centers where returning citizens are mandated to work-release programs and get outside employment to prepare for their return. The first time I went to recruit participants, I got in front of sixty inmates in three groups, forty men and twenty women. I discussed with them the hurdles they would face and the reasons many of them would be back. I told them, "It is not a matter of whether you want to return. I don't think any of you do. I also don't believe any of you are planning to come back, but the fact is, two out of every three of you will, unless you change your minds. If you keep doing the things you've always done, then you'll keep getting what you always get." I continued, "What if someone came and made you the following offer—upon release, we will give you a full-time job, a mentor, free housing for six months, if needed, a support group, fifteen free online life-skill classes, support for recovery, if needed, and if you can make it for six months with no problems, then we'll give you a scholarship to a local technical college to learn a trade. How many would be interested?" Every hand shot up.

We are taking away their excuses. On that day we took a sign-up list along with materials outlining the program. How did we do? We batted a thousand, as every single inmate wanted a shot and signed up. These men and women are hungry, and most will rise to the occasion if given a chance. We all deserve a second chance. We can find willing employers, housing developments, and technical colleges who are willing to help. And here is one of the coolest parts of the program: Some of our mentors happen to be police officers. Now that is a story our nation desperately needs right now. Let's give these returning citizens a shot, and let the ones who locked them up help them to stay free.

A Returning Citizen with His Cop Mentor

Politicians Soft on Crime

Judges, sheriffs, and other elected officials typically get elected and re-elected by "tough on crime" platforms. That is understandable, as they are trying to protect our communities.

That's what the public wants to hear, that they'll be safe and the bad guys will be locked away, out of sight, out of mind, and far from us. "Tough on crime" has come to mean longer time for lesser crimes and mandatory minimums for those who scare us. We have seen tougher sentencing, harsher treatment, and more prisons built as a result. A former commissioner of the department of corrections once told me, "There are two kinds of people in prison—the ones we're mad at and the ones we're afraid of. We need to keep the ones we're afraid of, and rehabilitate and release the ones we're just mad at" (violent offenders vs. nonviolent offenders).

But are politicians really tough on crime? We all most likely would agree that the current system is not effective at protecting our communities. Prisons are overcrowded; the average age of inmates is getting younger and younger; offenders are coming home more violent than when they went in; gangs are having their way and recruiting heavy on the inside, so more gang members are being released; the revolving door is releasing dangerous criminals back onto the streets to reoffend, and then they're coming back inside. Nobody can deny those realities. I believe we need to look at some of the state-mandated programs and the millions of dollars being spent that are not only failing, but wasting taxpayers' money on programs that are oftentimes, though unintentionally, making things worse.

When candidates campaign on "tough on crime" platforms but continue spending taxpayer money on programs that are unproductive and ineffective, we might conclude that today's politicians are actually soft on crime, without even knowing it. If we continue to send these brothers away for longer and longer sentences and fail to give them the proper treatment and care they are entitled to, then they become more violent behind the wire before returning to the same streets. It's time to take a hard look at what's not working and become willing to try some new ideas and out-of-the-box approaches.

The POPP Brothers in Muskegon

The Young Bloods

Here is a paradigm shift for politicians who want to remain tough on crime. We could focus on true rehabilitation, which would produce healthier and safer communities as inmates return. Here is an example.

The POPP celebrations are so inspiring and do almost as much for the inmates as the program itself. This is where they get a chance to shine. Imagine a brother who has never accomplished anything of real value or been recognized for anything positive in his life. Then he stumbles upon a program that challenges him to become the person he always dreamed he could be and gives him the tools to carry it out. This same program helps him build healthy relationships with men he fears, and also helps him build self-esteem. Imagine that same brother getting a chance to stand up in front of his peers and staff, and show them the brilliance he has discovered inside himself. Can you see why the demand for this program is so high in the prisons where we operate? This is why over half of the men in some prison populations have signed up for the Power of Peace Project.

At one of our prisons in Michigan, we were right in the middle of one of the most inspiring POPP graduation celebrations we have ever had. The men had just eaten like kings, as we brought in free-world food with all the fixings. Most of these men hadn't eaten like this in years. That alone was enough to draw many of them to the program in the first place, but then they caught something they didn't anticipate. They had just received their Certificates of Achievement, and they were treated to a spiritual hip-hop concert with a group we were traveling with out of Detroit. As the brothers danced, laughed, and sang, one particular group in the back got especially energized.

These were young Blood gang members who had been quite a challenge throughout the project. Oftentimes, early in the program, they were disrespectful and talked while other brothers were speaking. This brought them glares and rebukes from some of the other brothers, as they don't typically allow disrespect toward a free-world volunteer. However, they made progress throughout, and that is all we expect. This is a program of progress, not perfection. This is what the celebration is all about. We reward them for the progress they have made, whether it be heroic changes or baby steps in the right direction.

At one point in the celebration, this group of young, rambunctious Bloods broke from their table in the back and headed toward the front. I was on stage with the rap group and noticed them coming my way. My first thought was, *Why are they coming after me? I'm the peacemaker!* But then I noticed the expressions on their faces. They weren't angry or determined; they were laughing like kids, even joyful. When they got close, I braced for whatever was coming next. They proceeded to hug me, pick me up, and playfully push me around, almost like crowd-surfing! What I was witnessing was pure jubilation and a fascinating display of respect, but in their own unique way.

I wonder if they could have ever imagined, just forty days earlier, that they would be celebrating their victories in this way along with all their rivals. The power of incentive, reward, and positive reinforcement cannot be overstated, and I believe it is the answer. It has the potential to turn young, dangerous gang members into brothers striving to become better, even if they still have a long way to go. It's a positive start and proves there is still hope for this young, misguided generation.

In the next act we will focus on the tactics of the enemy, the incarcerated mind, mental health behind the wire, and how we rewire the convict brain.

Act Three

CHEWY'S REDEMPTION

Jesus a.k.a. "Chewy"

One of the first brothers I met in my very first prison in Georgia was a man named Jesus (his nickname is "Chewy"). The first thing that stuck out was that he happens to be a small man, which can be a real challenge unless you are affiliated with a gang, which he was not. Chewy is from Mexico and caught a life sentence in Georgia in 1994. I met him in 2009. He was working as the chaplain's orderly at the time, which is a good detail, but has its drawbacks. You can be wrongly tagged as a "snitch" when you have jobs where you work closely with staff. In prison, it is very much an "us against them" mentality, and being labeled a snitch can be deadly.

In most prisons across the country, Hispanic brothers hang together for protection because they are typically outnumbered. Beefs on the street are put on hold behind the wire, and rivals become brothers for a time. The pressure to affiliate can be intense because the consequences of not joining can be even worse. But Chewy never gave in, so life was hard for him the first ten of his twenty-five years. I always admired that about him, because I knew it took incredible courage and inner strength to go it alone. As he walked across the yard one day, all alone, I asked a brother, "How can Chewy survive in a prison like this when he is small and unaffiliated?"

The brother said, "Chewy is so spiritual that nobody dares touch him." I had never heard that before. Chewy and I became good friends.

Chewy had not always been the spiritual man I met. He was charged, convicted, and sentenced to life in prison for a murder he committed in 1994. Honor and respect are paramount in his culture, and reputation is everything. One night in a club a man publicly disrespected his wife in front of many witnesses, and her honor was on the line. This man put his hand on her backside and then said, "What are you gonna do?" He already had a beef with this man from an earlier altercation. Chewy made a decision he can never take back, one he regrets to this day. He left, got his cousin, and came back and killed the man who had dishonored his wife. He fled and was apprehended in Texas just before he got to the border.

Chewy was now in the Georgia Department of Corrections, sent from one maximum-security prison to another, which is the norm for high-security life-sentence prisoners. He had to figure out a way to earn respect and protection without affiliating with a prison gang. The men he grew up with in his hometown were connected to the cartels. He wasn't going back to that lifestyle, but he had to survive. So, he chose the drug trade, and he became very good at it.

Many in the free world wrongly assume it's hard to get drugs in prison. They couldn't be more wrong. Drug trade is huge in the prisons. The only difference is that drugs are much more expensive behind the wire. Chewy became a major player, and he got the respect he needed to stay protected. He organized a system to get the drugs smuggled in, and even had drugs flowing into other prisons as well. His influence made him a powerful man. You would be surprised what a drug hustle can earn you behind the wire—it's in the tens of thousands of dollars, which can bring you easy and safe time if you run it right. Chewy did just that.

Eventually there were allegations, and Chewy wound up in the hole for five months with nothing but time to reflect. He soul-searched and thought about his life. With no one to teach or counsel him, he turned his life over to God all by himself. He came out of solitary a changed man. But was it just jailhouse religion? Many in the free world judge inmates and say things like, "Yeah, of course they found God in there, because they had no other way to go." Isn't that when people tend to find God in the free world, when all other hope is gone? Maybe the brothers behind the wire are closer to redemption than many religious people out here.

He called his guys together and told them to bring him all the "ice" (a form of methamphetamine) he had before he was sent to the hole. They brought it to him, an amount worth approximately

$10,000. While they thought he was going to divvy it up to resume their hustle, instead, he flushed it down the toilet. They were obviously upset, and Chewy said to them, "These drugs are mine, aren't they? Then I can do with them whatever I please." And he flushed $10,000 down his prison toilet. He proceeded to order his guys to get the word out to anyone who still owed him money, which was a significant number of inmates, and tell them that whatever was owed was now forgiven. This is unheard of in prison. He had been thoroughly converted while in solitary.

But now the real work would begin. Once again, Chewy had to establish a reputation and earn respect as if he were a new convict. In the prison system, you must earn the right for people to respect your faith and conviction; it is definitely not a free pass. Many try to use their religion as a shield, thinking people will leave them alone if they love God. That absolutely is not the case. As a matter of fact, you can become even more of a target because it is seen as a weakness. Church inside a prison is where lots of business is conducted, and it's also a place for homosexuals to meet. So, going to church is not always a good move. However, if a brother has true faith that he is willing to stand up for, and even fight for, then he can earn the respect he seeks. I know a brother in an Ohio prison who was willing to get "stomped out" by the Aryan Brotherhood, which is a way to leave the gang, because of his faith and conviction. They call that "blood in, blood out." Sometimes brothers die during these rituals, but if you survive, you are free. Prisoners respect courage, and they can tell right away if your faith is not genuine. I wonder how many in the free world would be exposed as frauds under such circumstances.

Some of his former associates began to "try" Chewy and test his convictions. There were threats, challenges, and outright assaults as he began his new way of life. I asked him how he survived and won their respect, and his response was so powerful to me. He said, "I would tell them honestly, 'You don't want to make me into the man I used to be. You would much rather have me as the man of God I am today. If you force me to become the man I used to be, you will not like who I become. That man will not stop until you are dead.' And so, they left me alone." I was speechless.

I ran across Chewy several years ago in another prison he had been shipped to. He had a brand-new hustle and, once again, had established a formidable reputation. This time he had partnered with another man I know and respect named Martinez. Together, they started a church and had grown it to over 120 men. One Sunday, Chewy and Martinez took up a collection from their fellow prisoners. With the money they raised, Chewy fed the whole prison with food they normally wouldn't get, and his influence increased. These men are proving that they're going to make a difference one way or another, so let's give them the tools to make a positive change.

Years ago, I made a promise to Chewy. I told him if he ever got back to the free world, I would do everything I could to help him. He told me that upon his release, he would be deported back to Mexico and never allowed to return to the States, but I told him I would still do my best. I asked him where he was from, and he said Zihuantanejo. Immediately I thought of the movie *Shawshank Redemption*, and the scene at the end of the movie where Tim Robbins' character Andy Dufresne meets up with his friend Ellis "Red" Redding, played by Morgan Freemen, on the beach in Zihuantanejo, Mexico. I asked him, "You mean the place in Shawshank?" He smiled and said yes, that was his home. I told him that one day we would recreate that scene on the beach, but I had no idea if and when he would ever get out, as the parole board kept setting him off.

I recently got a call from Mexico. It was Chewy, but he had to leave a voicemail. He simply said, "Hello, Kit. It's me, Chewy. I am free and back in Mexico. I want to talk to you." Then he said, with tears, "You never treated me like a prisoner. You always treated me like a friend. I wanted to say thank you and I love you." I was overwhelmed with emotion when I got the message. After twenty-five long, hard years, Chewy had earned his freedom. I called him back and we talked for an hour and a half. I asked him how he and God were doing, and in his humble voice he said, "Oh, Kit, me and God are good friends. We love each other so much." I wish other Christians could see Him that purely and simply.

We are currently making plans for me to fulfill my promise. I'll never watch *Shawshank Redemption* through the same lens again, but now I call it "Chewy's Redemption." God bless my friend Jesus.

Chapter Nine
THE DARK SIDE IS ORGANIZED

Many think the dark side has no strategy, no real plan, and that it runs recklessly and out of control like we see on the streets, in movies, or on TV. That couldn't be further from the truth. Some gangs are hard to predict and have little structure, while others are organized and have sophisticated business plans. Until we develop effective strategies to rescue our kids from being preyed upon or recruited by gangs, these criminal organizations will continue winning this battle for the hearts and minds of our youth.

The Gangster Board Meeting

Years ago, in one of the maximum-security prisons I was serving in, a trusted brother gave me a phone number on a tiny piece of paper. He said, "You really want to understand the game? Call that number Sunday night at seven o'clock." That Sunday, out of curiosity, I called in at 7:00. I figured it was a conference call of some kind, but I didn't know what type of organization it was. Maybe it was a church, or a nonprofit, or perhaps it was an organization that helped prisoners, like Prison Fellowship.

When I jumped on the call, I heard people logging on with little beeps as more and more people joined the line. The participants were muted until the facilitator started the roll call. There were about thirty people on the line. The names seemed a little strange to begin with, but I didn't think much about it. It soon became obvious that it wasn't your typical conference call. It sounded something like this: "Red Dog?" "Here." "Chain Gang?" "Here." "Chicago?" "Present." And so on. I became aware that these were state prisons, and these were the gang leaders having their weekly conference call. My heart raced as I imagined what the consequences would be for being on this call as a civilian. I considered hanging up, but wondered when I would ever get an opportunity to see behind the curtain like this again. There is a world of darkness that the free world never gets to see, and it is more organized than you can imagine.

If I hadn't known what the group was, and had to guess just by listening, I would have thought it was a corporate call discussing bylaw changes, organizational structure, and current initiatives. It was that and much more. As I listened on high alert, they discussed monthly taxes, collection processes, and conflict resolution. The leader talked about when you could and when you couldn't put your hands on a brother, and how to handle violations with rivals. He discussed rule changes when it came to collecting past-due fees, and how to handle disagreements. Changes had been handed down from on high in the free world.

About halfway through the call there was another beep. Everyone went silent and the leader said, "Whoever just came on, please identify yourself." Silence. He spoke up once again: "Brother, identify yourself." Again, nothing but silence. Then he said, "You better say your name, brother." After more silence, the leader said, "Red, red, red." And I heard a series of beeps as thirty people jumped off the call, including me. I sat there with my heart racing after I hung up. I assumed they had been compromised and an officer must have confiscated an illegal cell phone. I had just witnessed how organized the darkness is. There was no profanity, no interruptions, and no yelling or arguing. It was strictly business, with a clearly defined agenda, handled in a professional manner. These weren't just prison gangsters and street thugs; these were businessmen, and it was all about the money and their code.

Why are we losing more and more of our young people to the streets? Because those who are winning are more organized, more committed, and more persistent than we are when it comes to recruiting our youth. They have a clear strategy, well-defined rules, and the funds to carry them out. In many ways our kids are getting more love from the streets than they are from the local church on the corner.

Gangs in Our Schools

I was recently on a Zoom call with a district attorney, a local president of the NAACP, and seven police chiefs from an influential county in my state. We were discussing ideas and practices around police brutality and systemic racism. We talked about training practices, use-of-force standards, and vetting officers. Then the issue of youth gangs came up, and the NAACP president asked if gangs were operating in our schools. I was surprised by the question, but ready for the chiefs to give their expert opinions. The consensus was that they were certain there were gangs in the high schools, but they weren't sure as to the extent. Law enforcement sees the wreckage of gang activities and brings strong cases against gang members, but are sometimes unaware of their strength and presence in our schools, especially the ones in the suburbs, where they operate more under the radar. This is no longer just an inner-city thing.

I spoke of the ideal candidates for gang life: kids who come from broken homes and single-parent households; kids grieving the loss of a family member, a friend, or a divorce; kids who are talented but not connected to a strong peer group; wounded kids and survivors of abuse; kids in foster care; and kids who are starving for love, acceptance, and a place to belong. Basically, they prey on kids who are disconnected and feel all alone and afraid. These young people are easy pickings for the gangs who offer everything they're looking for.

What scared, wounded, and lonely kid wouldn't want what they are offering? They'll give you instant family, protection, popularity, money in your pocket, shoes on your feet, clothes on your back, and girls to hang with, and they'll never, ever leave you. That's a whole lot more than our communities are offering. And here is the scary part: The gangs are identifying kids who have talent by the age of seven, and beginning to court them and groom them so they'll be ready to be "jumped in" by the time they reach twelve or thirteen. Yes, there is definitely a gang problem in our schools, and they are winning because they have a better strategy and, in many ways, are more committed, focused, and determined than we are.

The Story of Luis

My journey into the US prison industrial complex began with the request of a mother for her son. In 1998 I was leading a church outside of Atlanta, where I came to know a young man named Luis. He was about twelve or thirteen when I met him, and I became something of a big brother to him. He would wait in line to see me after my sermons and tell me what he had learned. He was a little bigger than the other kids, and had big brown eyes and a smile that would light up the room. He impressed me because none of the other boys his age would come to me, much less have anything spiritual to share. I imagined what he would do with his

The New Convict Code

life, but I knew he would most likely be a leader. When I moved on to lead another church in another town, I lost connection with Luis. Ten years later, his mother looked me up on Facebook and asked if I could go and see her son, because she knew he had always admired me. I responded that I would definitely go see him and asked what he was doing now. This was in 2008. She said that he was locked up on a serious charge and that she was heartbroken.

As I drove to the jail that night, I thought of my young friend Luis and tried to imagine what he looked like now. I wondered what he had done. As I waited in the visitation room, I hoped he would remember me, and I imagined that the same thirteen-year-old boy would walk in just as I remembered him. That wasn't the case. Who walked out was a grown man covered in tattoos with big dark eyes that looked like they had died, almost like shark eyes. But he recognized me, and his eyes brightened and that big smile I remembered flashed across his face. We hugged and then we talked, and talked, until they told me my time was up.

It broke my heart to hear his story. After I had left him when he was younger, he started high school in a fairly good area of town. He didn't have many friends, and he was picked on from time to time by kids who didn't look like him. He happens to be Hispanic. The girls weren't interested, and he was tired of being teased, so he gravitated to a group of kids that were more like him. In high school, everyone is trying to figure out where they belong and where they feel accepted and most comfortable. That's all he did. Within no time he had cool kids paying attention to him, girls he was talking to, and everyone who had picked on him was leaving him alone. This all seems quite normal, and even healthy, unless you know who his new peer group was. They are called MS-13.

MS-13 came to the States from Central America, mostly from El Salvador, Guatemala, and Honduras. By way of California they began to spread across the country, and today they have thousands of soldiers in communities throughout the US. Targeted by the FBI and the White House, they have become enemy number one when it comes to national criminal organizations. They are widely known as the most violent and brutal of street gangs; they prefer to use knives and machetes rather than guns, if possible, because it is more personal. They will kill anyone to advance their territory and power, whether it be civilians, children, judges—whoever gets in their way. They terrorize neighborhoods and are hard to predict. Luis was just looking for a place to belong and some friends he could fit in with. He had no idea what he was getting himself into.

He was the perfect target: big, smart, talented, good-looking, and all alone. Imagine the rush for a kid who was experiencing some drama at a new school. Cool kids putting money in your pocket, inviting you to parties, and introducing you to girls. The fact that these were "bad boys" made it even more alluring, because the girls seemed to like that. Next came alcohol, drugs, sex, and fighting. The whole thing can be quite intoxicating for kids who don't feel like they fit in anywhere else. And if you get that little feeling like something isn't quite right, it is easily overshadowed by all the things you are receiving that you've always wanted: attention, belonging, protection, and validation. Not long after that, he was officially jumped in. This is an initiation ritual where the new member is put in a circle with four, five, or more other gang members and beaten for thirteen seconds, or for as long as the other members choose. Luis told me because he was a little bigger, they put older, bigger guys in his circle. He fought with all his might and took a beating, but made quite an impression.

He chose his new nickname, "Pancho," and his gangster career was officially launched.

Luis was built for this from the start. He quickly figured out that courage and fearlessness paid big dividends in this new world, and he became the kid who would do just about anything. When they had meetings on Saturdays giving out work to be done, he would sit by the window so he could jump out and finish the assignment before anyone else, even the ones the work had been assigned to ("work" is criminal activity). That got him in trouble every now and then, but he gained a reputation as an earner and a wild card. In this world, that gets you promoted, and eventually Luis had his own crew. What made him successful as a gangbanger would have served him well in any other field he might have chosen, whether it was athletics, a trade, education, or anything else he put his mind to. He had courage, ingenuity, a strong work ethic, leadership skills, resourcefulness, and determination. It was just misguided. He was the perfect mark. What they fail to tell you when they recruit you is how much it will cost. Everything costs something, and this cost Luis everything.

One night in a small motel room, a drug deal with a rival went bad and someone lost their life. Luis was charged, and now he sat in front of me in a visitation room facing a potential death penalty from a federal government who has had it with this dangerous, bloodthirsty gang. They were out to make an example of my little brother. Twenty-six known MS-13 soldiers were rounded up, and Luis became the star witness as the only legal citizen in the group. The feds flipped him and he decided to cooperate, which meant he now had a contract on his head for the rest of his life. I would go on to work with him over the next two years as they sent him from facility to facility, along with all his former brothers, while the case dragged on and on. I taught him through the glass about the good life, and he taught me about the gang life. I learned things civilians never get to know about life on the dark side. Luis was invaluable to my work.

It took over seven years for him to go to trial, as the feds were not about to lose this case. He was in protective custody for those last couple of years before he finally went before a federal court judge. I met with his capital case attorney and provided information about his transformation in hopes of avoiding the death penalty. I stood and testified for him and pleaded with the judge for leniency as I explained all he had done to help me with my work. Between the time I first reconnected with him and when he finally went to trial, four years had passed, and my prison peace movement had spread from Georgia to the Midwest. Because of his good work helping so many, the judge gave him twenty years instead of the thirty he had been offered, as well as credit for time served. It is 2020 as I am writing this, and he will be home in five years. And I will be waiting for my little brother Luis, because I owe him.

Scared Straight vs. Inspired Straight

In the late seventies there was a popular TV show called *Scared Straight*. Kids who were getting into trouble were taken into jails and lined up in front of real inmates. The inmates would come in and try to scare the kids. They would yell in their faces, cuss and taunt them, tell them what they were going to do to them, and try their best to scare the hell out of them as a way to get them to change their path in life. There was little to no success. In my experience, telling people what might happen to them if they don't change their behavior does absolutely no good, and can actually have the opposite effect. Kids already have enough threatened consequences thrown in their faces, and they are hard to scare these days. I have seen it ignite the darkness inside of some kids.

In 2011, I took a group of teens to a maximum-security prison in North Georgia, but our program was called Inspired Straight rather than Scared Straight. We had a couple of our POPP inmates prepared to make a presentation to the kids. Snoop and Grimlock, who facilitated the event, are trusted brothers and friends to me, and my son was one of the participants. These kids weren't getting into trouble, though some eventually would. They were just average kids who were going to participate in an experiment with the permission of their parents. The talk went great as Snoop shared about his life and what led him to prison. Grimlock shared about life on the chain gang, and what he wished he would have known growing up. There were parts that were scary and shocking, and also parts filled with laughter and a few tears. They told stories, and the kids listened. They took questions, and the discussion went deep. They related to what these boys were going through, but also told them where certain thinking and behavior would take them.

Then we took them to the hole. This is where men are sent when they get into trouble or when they need protective custody if there is a credible threat. We wanted to give the boys a look into solitary confinement, which few people ever see. The boys were all lined up in the yard before we were to file into this building. As they stood out in the sun, some of the men began to see them through the slats in their windows. They began to shout to the boys from their solitary cells: "Give me the one in yellow!" one man shouted. "No, I'll take the one with the long hair!" another yelled. A strange vibe settled in among the boys as they prepared to enter. As we marched them around the inside of the building and by the cells, the inmates banged on the iron doors, causing quite a racket. The boys nervously laughed and tried to make light of it, but they were scared. We walked them around and let them talk to some of the guys through the small slots in their doors. The inmates encouraged some of them and tried to drop a little knowledge on them. They tried to get them to change before they made a mistake they could never take back. Most of these men really do want to help kids change their ways; they've just never been given a voice.

However, one inmate began challenging one of the boys and threatening him, kind of like *Scared Straight*, and other boys started watching. This aroused the darkness in this young brother, and he began to taunt the inmate back. This escalated the confrontation, and they began to challenge one another. We shut it down. We took the boys back to the front gate and made our way back to the bus. As you can imagine, the young brother who stood up to the gangster was "the man" all the way home. Now he had a story to tell all his friends, and any good that had been done in the Inspired Straight portion of our program was lost and forgotten.

Trying to scare this young generation almost always backfires, because they live in this virtual "hip-hop gangster" world where everything is about street cred. If we challenge them with threats and consequences, it often awakens something inside of them that we don't want to see. We are challenging them—and almost daring them—to show us how tough they are.

Inspired Straight, on the other hand, always works. Even if the seeds don't bear fruit right away, these kids will never forget what they saw and what they heard, and perhaps they will remember when their time of testing comes. Our kids need inspiration these days more than ever. Where else are they getting it? They're not getting it from their friends, social media, or video games, and they're rarely getting it from their parents or teachers. They might get some from their coaches, but only if they happen to be athletes, and very few are getting it through pastors or youth ministers. So, what we have with this young generation is a lack of inspiration. We are created to be inspired, and nothing else fills that void in the same way. Inspiration feeds the spirit, which is much different than motivation or education. Let us inspire them through transformed criminals who already have their respect.

Chapter Ten
THE INCARCERATED MIND

Human beings were never designed to live in cages. We were created to be free and to dream, build, grow, and thrive. When a man or woman is incarcerated, the mind changes, as it is now confined. Choices are taken away, the walls close in, and routine becomes everything. Less daylight, less human connection, and poor nutrition takes a toll on the brain and the mind suffers. The mind sees things it cannot unsee, and mental health deteriorates as hopelessness sets in. Terrifying sounds in the night and unbearable loneliness eventually take their toll, and the mind operates more like a creature trying to survive and forgetting about everything else that used to be important. They call this the chain-gang mind.

Mental Incarceration in the Free World

What I call mental incarceration is not only for convicts, but is more and more prevalent today in the free world too. We live in a heavily medicated society. While I believe there are vital, life-saving medications on the market, I think we can agree that things are spinning out of control in the pharmaceutical world. Big Pharma is producing more and more drugs to treat the side effects of all the other drugs they are producing and pushing on us. It is a machine, and greed is what fuels it. In many ways the pharmaceutical companies are becoming like drug cartels, the insurance companies like moneymen, the pharmacies like trap houses, and doctors like local pushers. We are seeing epidemic levels of addiction, depression, anxiety, suicide, overdose, violence, and many other forms of mental illness. Our brains are being bombarded with more stimuli than we can handle—way too much noise, way too much distraction, way too much drama. We are being stressed and stretched beyond our limits, and our minds are starting to show many signs of the same things I've been seeing behind the wire for a very long time. Perhaps some of the solutions laid out in this book could work in the free world as well. I believe they can.

Let's hear from my brother Sir Brown about mental incarceration behind the wire.

The Wisdom of Sir Brown

It's sad to witness a person with mental-health issues behind these walls. After many years of living among them, you can find sympathy or even empathy for them. My first encounter was at Valdosta State Prison. One dorm houses mental-health inmates who are basically nonviolent. They rarely bathe, or have to be given incentives to do so, receiving gifts ranging from cigarettes and coffee to sweets. Some talk to themselves, walk in circles, make outbursts, or even masturbate in public. Other dorms house violent mental-health inmates. They fight each other and the guards regularly. Most are given medications once or twice a day. Many cut themselves. It's normal to see men with arms, legs, faces, and necks scarred from self-inflicted wounds. The mental-health staff members are surprisingly attentive and patient. Suicide attempts occur often. Some are successful. I am not familiar with all the medicine administered, but there is an injection some violent men are mandated to receive that lasts thirty days per shot. There are levels mental-health inmates are classified to, ranging from one to four. On average, most are among levels one and two. Some are extreme athletes. Many have no idea what they're doing out there, and there are events that cater only to the mental-health caseloads.

Each inmate is given an ID card and a schedule that must be in our pockets at all times. The schedule has your daily itinerary: classes, name, inmate number, housing unit, and cell assignment. Even top or bottom bunk placement. The schedule will also show security and mental-health level. Not many facilities mix up general-population inmates with the serious mental-health inmates. However, an inmate can experience a mental breakdown due to pressure, death in the family, or abandonment of loved ones, and may be designated "mental health" for a certain evaluation period. Some have mental-health issues but have never been diagnosed. Some are in denial. I was told an insane person never questions his own sanity. And asking to be evaluated or seek psychiatric help is a sign of weakness, so many never inquire. Mental-health inmates can get cheated or taken advantage of. They get charged exorbitant interest rates, which they readily agree to for commissary items.

The Institutionalized Brain

The average person in the free world is going to make approximately 250 choices today, whether it be what to wear, what to eat, which store to go to, who to spend time with, etc. On the other hand, the average inmate is only going to make about twenty-five choices. Most of their daily decisions will be made for them: when to get up, when to shower, when to shave, when to eat, what to eat, who they can spend time with, what job they will have, when they will work, what products they can purchase, what recreational activities they can participate in, who can visit them and when, and so on. Now think about what that does to the brain.

When you remove choices, the brain locks into patterns and goes on autopilot. This is why inmates have such a hard time when they come out. They literally have hundreds of choices flying at them at once, and their brain gets overloaded and eventually shuts down. The longer they have been behind the wire, the more challenging decision-making becomes when they are set free. We call this being institutionalized. We often find the same thing with those leaving the military—many choices are made for them, and life in the free world becomes overwhelming. Many break under the pressure.

These days many schools, especially in underserved areas, are treating kids like convicts. They are told where to go, when to go, how long to be there, when to speak, when to be silent, when to move, when to sit still, when to eat, when to go to the bathroom, and so on. More and more choices are being taken away and they are becoming institutionalized, just in a different way.

Many schools have metal detectors at the entrances and the doors remained locked, and the food is less and less healthy. Little, if any, incentive is built in, but more and more punitive measures are being used every day. If you violate a rule, you are sent to in-school suspension. If you cause trouble, you get suspended. Little learning occurs, and the kids are becoming more and more restless. Eventually, many turn sixteen and hit the streets, already somewhat institutionalized. With too much time on their hands, they end up getting in trouble, and the cycle repeats. They are now caught up in a system that is hard to get out of, and their brains have been prepared for prison life by the schools where they have *done their time*. If we don't change the way we're educating our kids, more and more of them will continue lining up for prison.

Trapped inside a Mental Cage

Many of these brothers are truly sick and are trapped in the cage of their diseased minds. I want to start by saying this section is a bit difficult for me to write, because it deals with sensitive subject matter.

I was involved in a weekend event at one of our institutions with about fifty inmates in a maximum-security prison. It was a three-day event, and I was there as a spiritual advisor if any of the men needed private counsel. During one of the breaks, a brother approached me and asked if we could have some individual time, as he needed help with something. He seemed anxious. I said yes, and we found a place away from the rest of the inmates in the gymnasium we were using.

We sat face to face, and he began to share with emotion the struggle and pain he was dealing with. He told me about his life and about the abuse he endured as a child. He spoke of his numerous prison terms and how he was now doing a long sentence for the crimes he had committed. Tears fell as he told me the nature of his crimes and his inability to stop. His crimes involved children, and he was repeating the terrible things that had been done to him. He was not justifying or excusing his horrible addiction, but he was expressing his immense guilt and shame, and his sincere desire to change and be done with his evil desires. He wanted to know if forgiveness was achievable and if deliverance was even a possibility. My heart went out to him, although his crimes were repulsive. Was there hope for a man this twisted? He desperately wanted to know. He began to cry and asked if I could pray with him, so we held hands and I began to pray. His tears moved me as well, and it was a sacred moment. Afterward, I gave him a hug, and he walked back to the group. While I couldn't relate to his problem, I could relate to his pain. I've never seen him again.

Compassion is such a powerful energy. It brings people together through common experience, even if it is just imagined. You can't fake it; either you feel what the other is feeling, or you don't. Through practice, we can learn to imagine what the other is feeling and what it would be like to be in their shoes. Empathy is even more powerful, as this occurs when we have actually experienced what the other is feeling. For instance, if someone comes to me in deep pain because they are going through a difficult divorce, I can have compassion for them, but not empathy, if I've never been through a divorce. On the other hand, if I have been through the same ordeal, and I can identify with that particular pain, then I experience empathy for them.

Many of the men I meet who have committed violent offenses, especially young inmates, invariably have a problem with empathy. Studies suggest there could be mental illness in the part of the brain that controls empathy. If I can hurt you without feeling any of your pain on some level, then there is a wiring problem in my brain. However, many who commit violent offenses can still experience empathy, depending on the motive driving their behavior. But when someone begins to enjoy inflicting pain, there is a serious underlying disorder. You have likely heard that one of the early signs in the lives of serial killers is hurting or killing animals. This is often where it begins, because these people have an illness that affects empathy. They do not identify with the pain they inflict. This is by no means an excuse; these people need to be separated from society to protect other potential victims.

So, as I sat with this man as he shared his horrible secret, my heart went out to him. I felt the pain of a man struggling with his nature, which I have experienced in my particular challenges.

Though I couldn't relate to his compulsion, I had compassion, and that was enough for a human connection. That is a place to start. If I can feel the other, or at least imagine what might be driving their behavior, then I can remove myself from the equation and focus on giving them what they need. People need to learn this crucial skill in today's climate of hatred and judgment. Maybe, just maybe, we could start to make progress toward reconciliation.

The Wisdom of Sir Brown

My mother used to say, "The mind is what the mind is fed." So, if you come from a spiritual background, you are preached to about that particular religion. Value systems are set in place, and a certain consciousness about right and wrong is usually your guide. A person born into a household of crime, neglect, and violence has a mind that's fed something totally different: survival. Lie, cheat, steal, rob, and manipulate.

All of these are totally acceptable in their world. The mind is what the mind is fed. Now, imagine an eighteen-year-old taking a bus ride to his first prison. Whether this kid comes from preachers or prostitutes, his imagination is spinning out of control. He's scared. You may not hear him admit that, but he is. Everyone has a certain fear of the unknown, regardless of age. He believes what he's seen in movies. He will be abused in some kind of way. He may have to kill someone. He should seek out the biggest person and attack him. He should go into protective custody. Reality hits, and it may be different for five different people arriving at the same time. One gets robbed. Another is asked where he is from and finds out he has homeboys who embrace him. Another is forced to join a gang. Another becomes a Muslim. Another finds solace in his Bible.

The first night, most barely sleep. You realize you are alone. You're hoping the friends and family you've left behind will stick it out with you. During mail call, you may receive none—not a postcard, greeting card, or letter. You understand most relationships are on life support and you may have to do all of your sentence alone. Bitterness can creep in. Anger can cloud your mind. Sadness may lead to depression as the mind unravels. If an event takes place that causes the facility to be locked down for a long period of time, the isolation can drive you even further into madness.

Prison is hard, extremely difficult to contend with. But for a young person, it's ten times worse. They can get influenced by the wrong elements and early on create situations and enemies that will keep popping up. For me, the key is gratitude. I mean, no matter what takes place, I can see the upside. We get locked down? That's an opportunity to study or write loved ones. Commissary is cancelled? That's an opportunity to fast or ration out my food. Yards are cancelled? Get some push-ups in the dorm. You get an unexpected injury? Maybe that's a sign your body needs to slow down. No one visited this past weekend? Remember the times when they did, or visit an old guy in your dorm and sit with him. I am no longer young, so I realize one of the keys to doing time is to develop a routine. But if the routine is broken, and it will be, learn to improvise. But mostly, be grateful. Gratitude is the key to everything.

There is a universal phrase in every prison: Commissary is necessary. Vital to incarcerated existence. On the inside, the world revolves around it. Same with life on the outside. Life is like a sandwich; no matter which way you flip it, the bread comes first. How you get it is up to you, whether you go to the commissary department and place an order or the local Walmart. They don't ask how you made the money. They say, "$69.99, please." We used to go to a window and pick up our purchases, but this created a challenge for some. You had to make it back to your dorm without getting beaten and robbed. So, the system got changed.

Commissary is now delivered to the dorms. Now all purchases are placed in a net bag in full view of ninety-five other guys. You can't always trust words, but you can trust patterns. Wild game is caught because of patterns. Migration patterns cause animals to be captured. Police catch criminals due to specific patterns. Many situations can be predicted due to patterns. So, behind these walls, your pattern of spending is carefully observed by those seeking to acquire what you have. Patterns—that's what it's all about.

If someone says they're going to do something for you and repeatedly does not come through, they can be hated like an enemy. And one of the worst things to hear is someone with resources saying, "I've been praying for you." Hands that help are holier than lips that pray. If an individual says, "I'm praying for you," but have nothing else to contribute, that's understandable. You can't give what you don't have. But it's a horrible and painful slap in the face when it comes from someone you know can change your situation. The only thing that matters is results. Everything else is just smoke and mirrors. Be it helping someone move, preparing a barbeque, sharing the driving on a long trip, rent money, painting, or visiting a sick or lonely person—imagine they need your help, but in the long run all you've done is say, "I've been praying for you." Patterns, results. Everything else doesn't mean shit.

Forty Years to Break the Cycle

After all the prisons and jails I've been in over the past ten years, I've only been injured once. I was participating in a program in a prison in the Midwest called Shakespeare Behind Bars. Tough inmates study, learn, and eventually perform Shakespearean tragedies as a way to connect with their pain and wounds, and learn to heal and become more peaceful. As we finished the session, I was making my rounds and saying goodbye to my friends, as I was heading back to Atlanta and wouldn't see them again for a couple of months. As I went around the circle shaking hands and hugging the brothers, a big, strong, tall man they called Harden-Bey came up from behind me and embraced me in a bear hug. That would have been fine, but he caught me unaware and grabbed me from an awkward angle. As he squeezed me, I felt something pop. I thought he had broken a rib, but it turned out I had only torn some cartilage. I had finally gotten hurt behind the wire, but it came as a result of love!

Mr. Harden-Bey left an indelible impression on me, and it wasn't from the torn rib cage. It was the transformation I witnessed over the three years I knew him. When we met, I knew him only as an enforcer for a group called the Moors, which is a sect of Islam prominent inside prisons in the Midwest. There is a large community of Muslims in Dearborn, Michigan, because many relocated there as refugees escaping the war in Iraq. There is a growing number of converts to Islam inside the prison system in America. My work with the Muslims has thus become very important, as they are a growing and influential segment in the prison industrial complex. They are built for a movement like ours because they are all about discipline, organization, and structure. Once I win the respect of their leadership, their soldiers become great peacemakers.

I saw Mr. Harden-Bey become a role model to younger inmates. He is an older man than I am, and he is large and imposing at first glance. He has a huge heart, but you can miss it if you only see his intimidating stature. He has been incarcerated for over forty years. Imagine going inside in 1979 and becoming eligible for parole in 2021. Think about how much the world has changed in the last forty years. It hasn't for him, nor for the hundreds of thousands of men doing long bids. Time stands still behind the wire. However, Mr. Harden-Bey used that time to break the cycle of violence and incarceration and become a living example to the young brothers of the change that is possible if they put in the work and invest in themselves.

Prison programs are so valuable to the inmates, as well as the free world. When a brother invests his time and energy in a program for at least two years, the recidivism rate for that inmate drops significantly. Is it that prison programs are all so effective and productive? Many of them are and many of them aren't. However, the fact that the inmates can feed themselves new information and invest in their well-being starts a momentum they carry with them into the free world upon their release. More healthy brothers being released into our communities equates to less crime and violence, and thus fewer victims in those communities. So, what is the answer to crime and violence in our streets? If we help brothers recover and heal from what's ailing them, they can continue to heal when they go home, and prayerfully raise the young ones on the streets who have no code.

That's what Mr. Harden-Bey has done, and he has been healed, even though it took forty years. I saw him stand in front of a hundred prisoners, many of them young, and say, "For years I was a violent man. At times I put steel into a man thinking I was strong. But now I see I was only a coward. All the violence in my life came from my fear. Now I am no longer afraid, and I have no need or desire for violence in my life." That is extraordinary. A strong, tough, feared man allowing himself to be vulnerable in front of his enemies and peers. He has participated in so many programs and earned so many certificates, and even a couple of degrees, while doing some of the hardest time the state could throw at him. He is now a role model to young inmates for how to do time, instead of letting time do them.

Recently I had the honor and privilege of standing up for my friend Mr. Harden-Bey at his parole hearing after four decades of incarceration. The parole board was impressed with his change and has recommended he be released. Now he will walk out into a world he doesn't know, but he will go home with passion and a purpose. He will help young people choose a different path than the one he chose. Many of our kids are most definitely ready to listen, and he has earned the right to speak.

Chapter Eleven
THE MENTAL BATTLEFIELD

Prisons are battlefields. Gangs run things and officers try to stop them. Fights happen daily, stabbings happen weekly, and killings can happen at any time. Robbery, extortion, and retaliation are routine, and things are only getting worse. So, if we intend to reform this flawed system, and we know many of the residents are motivated to change it, where do we start? If we can't change their thinking, we will not be able to change anything. However, if you can change a man's mind, you can change his life. Many have tried to change inmate behavior, but most times they fail because they haven't been effective in adjusting their thinking. I challenge them all the time: "If you keep thinking the way you always think, then you'll keep getting what you always get. Don't believe the lie that you'll never come back. If you continue thinking the same way you do in here, when you get out there, you'll be right back." When released, an inmate is taken to the bus station, given thirty-five dollars, and often told, "See you in six months." So, I developed a simple method to change their thinking in a way that would motivate them, while not overwhelming them.

The Fascinating World of Uncle G

Inmates love when I teach about "Uncle G." Though there are

many inmates who are highly educated, on average the typical prisoner has not completed his high school education, some have never learned to read or write well, and most have never been taught anything about how their brains work. However, they will listen intently for hours if someone feeds them valuable information. When I walk through the yard at POPP prisons, brothers will shout, "Uncle G!" in my direction and laugh and wave. They love knowing they have the power to rewire their brains for success and victory in a place where many brains are operating on a base level, merely trying to survive.

Years ago, I began studying science, as I am constantly trying to figure out why things are the way they are and how God designed everything we see today. That led me to cosmology and psychology, quantum physics and biology, and philosophy and world religion. The study of energy blew my mind, and from there I journeyed into brain science. I decided to figure out a way to teach some basic fundamentals of the brain to kids as well as prisoners. I also wanted to use it in churches as well as corporate gigs. I created a character I call "Uncle G" to represent the brain. I call him Uncle G to remind myself I am not him and he is not me.

The brain, while incredibly sophisticated and wonderfully complex, and having almost unlimited potential, is still merely an organ. Just like my liver or my spleen, my pancreas or my lungs, my heart or my kidneys, the brain is an organ created to help me survive and thrive. However, unlike my other bodily organs, this one can talk to me, reason with me, justify and persuade, rationalize and minimize. All day long this organ speaks to me in my own voice and reasons with me to get me to do the things I always do in the same way I always do them. He attempts to get me to hold on to the precious habits and patterns I have trained him, by repetition, to protect. Uncle G is not built to make me happy, but rather to keep me alive. He is a survival machine designed by our Creator.

Why do I call him Uncle G? First, he is the original Google. Can you remember what we did before Google? It's a wonder we figured anything out. All I do is ask a question, and it gives me an answer. However, the answer is only as good as the quality of the question. Ask good questions, and you get good answers. Ask it for profane garbage, and it will oblige you. Ask it for wonderful and beautiful things, and it will not disappoint. If I type "babe" into the search string and hit enter, I am going to find some pretty raunchy things nowadays, which is a shame. Back in the day you would find beautiful infants and toddlers, or maybe a loveable pig. These days you're going to receive something completely different, so please don't allow your children to try this at home! However, if I simply add the word "Ruth" to the end of "babe," then all I will find is baseball and candy bars. The same is true with Uncle G. Ask him to find brilliant and beautiful things by repeated attention and focus, and he knows how to find more. But if you continue to focus on garbage, he will create habits around trash and seek more and more filth.

Second, Uncle G is the original GPS. I'm amazed how I found my way to any destination before we had GPS. We had huge atlases that couldn't even fit in the glove compartment. So, we did the only logical thing, which was to find the most brilliant person in town, who happened to work at the gas station, and inquire as to our desired destination. And we trusted them completely. "Go down this road and take your second left. Then drive a mile or so and take a right where that big tree used to be. It's down on the left a-ways." Really?

Now I simply type in the address and it takes me to those exact coordinates. Once again, the directions are only as good as the input. If I put in a vague location like "Atlanta," my GPS will most likely take me to the capitol building downtown. However, if I put in the address to Centennial Park, all I need to do is listen to the GPS lady's voice and she will direct me right to it. The quality of the input equals the quality of the output. It's the same with Uncle G. If I write down where I want to go, which are my plans, goals, and dreams, then Uncle G knows how to take me there. The more I review them, the more he gets it locked in, and he knows the coordinates to that particular destination.

Thirdly, Uncle G is the Original Gangster, if you let him be. Without clear direction and guidance, he likes to run things. He will find whatever you have trained him to find, and he will take you wherever you go the most. One time when I was taking my son to the movies, I had a clear destination in mind and the desire to get there. I had been there a hundred times, and it wasn't far from our house. As we drove, we got into a conversation, and my autopilot took over. There was a series of turns, exits, merges, and lights, but we continued to talk, and I continued to blindly follow Uncle G. I braked, put on my blinker, accelerated, and performed many other maneuvers. These were difficult maneuvers when I first learned to drive, but now those habits live in my subconscious, where all my other habits live. Finally, we arrived. Do you know where we were? It wasn't the theater, it was Starbucks. If not given enough information, Uncle G will take me where he thinks I want to go, based on where I go the most. He has learned over time that I like to go to Starbucks first. Habits are everything, so if you change your habits, you change your life.

Uncle G is a two-million-year-old device, and he carries the secrets of the Universe. His intelligence is ancient and built-in, the way our Creator designed it. He has all the answers, and he is perfectly capable of finding us whatever we need and taking us anywhere we want to go. Recently Elon Musk and his SpaceX program successfully took two astronauts into space and safely arrived at the Space Station, where they stayed for two months in a rocket his company constructed. Then they splashed down in the Atlantic Ocean, something NASA hasn't done for forty-five years. Elon did all that with his fascinating Uncle G. One day in the not-too-distant future we will take people to Mars. Uncle G has the ability to help us become whoever we want to be and take us wherever we want to go. We simply need to keep him fed with the content that keeps him running smoothly and efficiently, and be clear on where we want him to take us.

The brothers love learning about the reticular activating system. This is the part of the primitive brain that, among other things, is in charge of filtering information and allowing you to notice things as you go about your day. Whatever you have programmed Uncle G to notice, based on relevance, he finds and directs your attention to it. If we didn't have this tightly webbed net of neurons to catch and filter all the billions and billions of bits of information we do not need, then we would not be able to function, as we would be bombarded with too many stimuli. As it is, Uncle G continues to find and bring to our attention all the things he has learned are important and relevant to us. No two people see the world the same way, because each of us has programmed our RAS to find different things and see the world the way we have trained him to see it. We have all experienced this amazing part of our brain when we are in the market for a certain kind of automobile. We don't notice a particular make and model until we're in the market for that kind of car. Then, and only then, do we notice them all around us. Our RAS has quickly learned to find what we are looking for based solely on the fact we now care about it.

Uncle G does not judge; he merely finds what is important to me. He doesn't have a conscience, he doesn't differentiate between good and bad, healthy or unhealthy, safe or unsafe; he just seeks and finds what we are unconsciously looking for. He doesn't have a brain; he is a brain. He is not in charge of making me happy; he is designed to keep me alive. Habits and patterns are everything to him. As soon as he notices you are doing the same thing over and over, he creates a habit and moves it into the powerful subconscious, which guides your ship.

This is good news or bad news depending on what you regularly feed him. Addiction works in a similar way. The more you watch, listen, read, perform, play, taste, feel, or smell a certain experience, the sooner you build habits around that activity. Whatever Uncle G does often, he does well. And once he gets used to a certain substance or activity, he gets a taste for it and will begin to persuade you to give him more. He is persistent and persuasive, and the tricky thing is that he speaks in your voice throughout the day, trying to find you what he believes you really want. He's like that knucklehead friend who is always tempting you to do things that aren't necessarily good for you.

The Learning Machine

All day, every day, Uncle G is watching, listening, and learning. He is always paying attention to whatever we're paying attention to. We can't hide anything from him, and given enough time and access, almost nothing is out of his reach. He develops the habits that are beneficial, healthy, and helpful for you to be, do, and have the life of your dreams. He can also work against you to find the things and create the circumstances that can lead to your worst nightmares if he is unattended. It's all a matter of whether you are using him, or he is using you. Either he is in charge or you are in charge. I'm either managing him or he is managing me. This is where mindfulness is key. If I am present and aware throughout the day of what I am thinking and doing, staying present and focused on the task at hand, then I am in control and he is serving me as a competent partner and valuable advocate. When I am not present and just running on preprogrammed routines, then I am reinforcing those programs and being further programmed by the world around me.

Just consider how much Uncle G has learned about the way you do life. Your family has been a huge influence on how your brain has been wired and programmed. All of the following have combined to create your unique perspective, or lens, through which you see the world: the friends you've chosen, the role models you've had, your faith journey, your education, your hobbies, your romantic interests, your profession or the jobs you've had, your ethnicity and cultural influences, your successes and failures, and more.

Uncle G learns fast behind the wire. Almost everything becomes a perceived threat, and he is constantly on high alert. After years of real or imagined fight-or-flight, Uncle G has a hard time adjusting to the free world, much like a soldier returning from a battle zone. So, we teach the brothers to deliberately create time each day to direct their brain's attention to new things, and how to create peace in a world of turmoil. Learning the art of focused attention, meditation, and mental discipline is crucial for the brothers if they are going to have any real success assimilating when they return to society.

The Storyteller

As Uncle G learns, he begins to tell stories about the things he's been taught. This is the voice in your head who speaks to you all day long. Any story that rolls around in your head long enough can become a belief. Once it becomes a belief, it operates unaware in the subconscious mind. We all have little-boy and little-girl stories that stay buried deep inside of us as we grow older.

For example, an eight-year-old boy goes through his parents' divorce. An eight-year-old brain must make sense of it somehow, so it creates a story a little boy can understand. Maybe it goes something like this: "Things never last, and people always leave me." It matters not whether the story is true, but rather if it makes sense to his young mind. The truth is that some things don't last, and sometimes people leave. But to the mind of a child, it can become "always" and "never"—absolutes. Think about how that particular story can affect a life if unchallenged. After a series of failed relationships and self-sabotaging, the grown man discovers he has been driven by that eight-year-old mental construct. How can you truly have an intimate, fulfilling relationship when you have a core belief that things never last and people always leave you?

Or maybe Uncle G creates this story based on your thoughts, experiences, and the relationships that have been modeled for you: "I'm never good enough, and I'm not worthy of love." Maybe you feel as though you have good reasons and lots of evidence for that belief. Maybe a parent made you feel like you were unworthy and undeserving by constantly rejecting you or blaming you. So that story, if you tell it to yourself long enough, can set in as a core belief. Later in life, when you're all grown up, you might fear success or refuse to believe compliments or be unable to receive encouragement. These things lie in the deep and dark recesses of our minds.

Uncle G has been studying how you see the world, how you see people, and how you see yourself ever since you were old enough to become self-aware. You must listen to the voice in your head and challenge the stories Uncle G is telling. If he is not given new information, or new stories, then he will continue to tell the same tales he told yesterday and the day before. Most people are regurgitating the same content in their heads today as they did yesterday with no new material, just recycled patterns and habits of dialogue. Uncle G is a storyteller, so it's time to give him some new stories.

Imagine the stories these brothers have had going through their heads for a lifetime. What you believe is your reality, whether true or illusion. Together, we create new stories for them to tell themselves, stories that build self-esteem and self-worth.

The Dealer and the Junkie

The voice in our head, the stories we tell, along with our beliefs all drive the fascinating chemical world within our mysterious vessel. A belief, whether it is true or not, drives our chemistry. Here's an example: If someone ran into my office right now and yelled, "Your wife has been injured in an accident!" I wouldn't have to command my brain to send the signal so I would have the right chemistry to handle this crisis. It would do it automatically without even consulting me. Those eight words, in that particular order, would kick-start a rush of adrenaline, among other chemicals, so I would be prepared to run to the scene or confront whomever was causing my wife harm. Adrenaline is an amazing drug. It can give you superhuman strength, make you oblivious to pain, and heighten your awareness.

These things are important when faced with a real life-or-death situation, but what about when it's merely a story in my mind? What if I am constantly telling myself stories all day that cause worry, fear, and dread and continue to elicit that same adrenaline response? Many people today are operating that way. They are stuck in a constant state of fight-or-flight, and they are on the verge of snapping at any minute. We see this with road rage. It often has little to do with the perceived infraction, but rather the person's mental state at the time of an honest mistake.

Now, imagine you reside in a dangerous place where two thousand men live in close quarters where none of them want to be. There are actual threats around you constantly, and your brain is always on high alert. At every moment you are searching, if even unconsciously, for threats and potential danger. And every perceived threat kicks off another powerful adrenaline blast, whether it's real or imaginary.

The Three Amigos

Understanding that many inmates in the prison system struggle to read and write well, I had to create a method to teach basic brain science in a way they could understand and easily remember. So, I came up with creative characters to illustrate basic principles. This led to the story of Uncle G and his Three Amigos. The Three Amigos represent the neurotransmitters dopamine, serotonin, and adrenaline. I use cartoon characters to illustrate, in a simple way, what they do and how they help us. Adrenaline is pictured as a hulking muscle man who loves to fight, dopamine is pictured as a wild party guy, and serotonin is pictured as a peaceful little guru.

The first of the Three Amigos is the powerful drug known as adrenaline. I teach the brothers that adrenaline is triggered by our fight-or-flight response, and it gives us the ability to run fast or fight hard when there is a threat. We discuss how adrenaline plays a big part of prison life due to the perception that a threat lies around every corner, and it often does. The problem comes when we live in a constant state of fight-or-flight and we have a constant flow of adrenaline pulsing through our bodies. Too much of this Amigo leads to a variety of physical and mental problems, especially in an environment with so much depression, anxiety, and rage. Adrenaline puts the body on high alert and prepares us for drama or leads us to create it when there is none. Ever seen someone addicted to drama? The cells in our body actually become addicted to this powerful neurotransmitter and will create more opportunities to produce it. I teach the brothers to be aware of their state and realize when adrenaline is spiking so they can investigate whether there is indeed an active threat, or just psychological fear.

The second of the Three Amigos is dopamine. Dopamine is the neurotransmitter connected to pleasure and reward. Drug addicts chase the dopamine response triggered by cocaine, meth, heroin, and other drugs. Dope fiends aren't addicted to their drug of choice, but rather to the over-release of dopamine the drug produces in their brain. I teach the brothers that many things will produce that dope blast: Gambling, shopping, chocolate, porn, risky behavior, or even rage, just to name a few, can get you the blast you desire. It's the anticipation of reward that triggers the dopamine response. It's released at the moment the bet is placed, or as the dress is purchased. It's triggered when you pull up the screen, or as you're about to take the first bite of cake. It's the routine of the junkie as he ties up his arm for the injection, or when you are about to explode with rage. It's the anticipation of the pleasure reward that signals the brain to release that fascinating chemical that takes us to another state of mind.

Just think about how important dopamine is in a place like a prison. It is a momentary escape from the hell in which they live. That is why drugs are so prevalent and why they cost so much more behind the wire. The problem comes when we get hooked on dopamine from unnatural sources. The more we become dependent on this powerful drug, the more we need the next time to get into that same state. Then the addiction cycle is set—more and more stimuli is required each time to get the same dope response as the previous time. At the same time, the brain produces less and less of its own natural dopamine, as it has learned it will be triggered by outside sources. Uncle G always protects his supply by conservation.

The third of the Three Amigos is serotonin. Although not as sexy as the first two, this transmitter puts us into a state of calm and ease. When serotonin is at normal levels, we feel like everything is right with our world. When those levels run low, we can feel hopeless and everything looks bleak. Adrenaline and dopamine decrease levels of serotonin, which in turn drives an addict toward more pleasure-seeking activity. For example, the addict is driven to more drug-seeking behavior as he becomes more hopeless and depressed. It's a maddening cycle that leads to breakdown. You should see the lights come on in the brains of these men as they learn they are not crazy, and there is hope for the health of their brains. The brain is neuroplastic and will continue to rewire itself for the rest of our lives, based on what we feed Uncle G. Knowing this shows them they have much more control over their emotions and attitudes than they realize.

To combat these addictions, I show them natural ways to produce serotonin and dopamine, and decrease the adrenaline produced by psychological drama. For instance, when we perform a random act of kindness for a stranger, serotonin is released in our brains, often accompanied by goosebumps. The receiver of the kindness gets a dose as well, and even an observer of that kindness can get a shot. Everybody gets a sense of well-being and calm from one selfless act. Therefore, if I'm feeling anxious from self-induced drama, or feeling out of control from chasing too much pleasure, all it takes is some kindness toward someone and immediately my chemistry and energy shift. The brothers love to experiment with these techniques and try to "change their channel," as we call it—a good exercise when you have nothing but time and plenty of opportunity to work on stress, anxiety, and fear.

From there, it's an easy leap to activate their imagination with the following exercise. I have them visualize the energy coming out of their prison as a dark beam shining upward from the center, in between the razor wire. The turbulence and rage create a dark energy that shoots out of the prison toward the sky. Then we imagine one inmate at a time shifting his energy and turning his light on. As more and more lights turn on (we are looking down at the prison from above now), they begin to connect and overcome the darkness with light. This light wave spreads across the prison and eventually becomes a unified beam of light as violence decreases. It becomes a powerful shaft of blinding light exploding from the wire upward toward the heavens. Can you see it? You should feel the energy in the room shift as the brothers collectively imagine their points of light connecting and changing their environment.

Then I challenge them to *be* the light, not the darkness. I warn them not to snuff out another's flame, for they are only hurting themselves and turning where they live into a firestorm of adrenaline and rage. The guru signals dopamine that the party is over and sends adrenaline away as well, and peace comes. I just got goosebumps as I wrote these words. There's that little guru again.

Chapter Twelve
A SOLITARY LIFE

As much as 40 percent of the men and women locked up in our country struggle with some sort of mental illness. When you have a large group living in a cramped space, while not one of them wants to be there, and most of them are angry about it, things can get quite colorful. When you factor in spiking mental illness, just like we're seeing in the free world, then you have the perfect storm. That storm rages when privileges are taken away and human rights are denied. Our current broken system is punitive, as more of the prison population is being confined to their cells, with less and less physical activity or free time. This makes a horrible situation even worse. If things keep trending like they are now, we'll only keep building more and more prisons, and everyone will be in a state of perpetual lockdown.

Time in the Hole

Solitary confinement is common practice in corrections in America. When a prisoner breaks certain rules, they are sent to the hole. In one prison we worked with, offenders were being sent to solitary for nine months at a time before going back into the general population. This has devastating effects on the inmate's mind. Long-term solitary confinement is cruel and unusual because it takes away our most basic need: human connection. I have ministered to inmates in solitary many times, and the things I have seen would shock you. I have seen brothers completely in the dark, getting their meals through a tiny slot, and having to get on their knees to peer out of the slot in order to communicate. Many of these inmates already have undiagnosed and untreated mental illness, and confinement only exacerbates it. When they are released back into the general population, they come back hungry, angry, depressed, and desperate. That leads to more violence, more time in the hole, and the cycle repeats.

POPP Teens in an Ohio Juvenile Prison

POPP Youth Take a Stand

I was invited to bring my program to juvenile prisons in Ohio. It encouraged me, as they were looking for creative solutions to the growing number of hours these young men were being locked up in solitary confinement, and the effects it was having on violence in their youth facilities. In one institution, they had over six hundred collective hours in the hole in a given month, with a juvenile population of approximately 150 boys. That is a very high number and very destructive.

So, we launched a version of the same program that was

becoming so effective in the adult facilities where we operate. All the boys signed the peace pledge, and we set out on our Forty Days of Peace. There were basically two gangs that ran the place, and the leaders were natural enemies. They were both strong, smart, talented young men, but they were pitted against one another, and probably didn't even realize they had a choice. They fought every day, and their fellow gang members did the same. When they fought, they were sent to the hole.

These young gang leaders had to sit together each week as they worked through the program. The closer they were in proximity, the closer they became. By the end of the forty days, these two young men had become best friends, as kids typically do when they spend time together. They found that they had so many things in common, and many of the same strengths. The younger we are, the easier it is to make friends, because typically there is less ego in the way. They began to get advice from each other, and slowly but surely, the rest of the kids stopped fighting. Fewer and fewer kids were sent to the hole, and the number of seclusion hours went from over six hundred a month to less than a hundred during the months our program was running. This was a record in the state of Ohio. The warden and administration were responsible for these historic changes, but POPP was given credit as well, as this was the only program added during that stretch.

We had proven once again that inmates can and will change when properly motivated and given the tools to be successful. Even young men want to change.

Decency on Death Row

I've lost three friends to lethal injection, which can change your perspective on the death penalty. There are two death-row facilities in Alabama. One houses almost all inmates sentenced to die by capital punishment in the state, but the other has only twenty-four beds. Unlike any other death row I have seen, the warden at this facility allows the brothers to come out of their tiny cells for six to eight hours a day and hang out together in their little common area. This makes all the difference in the world. They have become a misfit band of brothers. I have seen their tears when another of their brothers is executed. I have seen inmate spiritual leaders teach the other men. The men who have serious mental-health issues do better than other inmates who suffer the same illnesses in the general population. Human contact and healthy camaraderie produce effective results and help these men have some kind of quality of life before they are taken from the planet.

Typically, it takes about twenty years to execute an individual in most states because they are entitled to three appeals. Can you imagine spending twenty years in an eight-by-ten cell with no one to commune with? You might be saying to yourself, "Well, they deserve it." I have a friend who died on death row several years ago who was not guilty. I know this because a former judge who visits the prisoners there told me that personally. He was very knowledgeable with the case and said that this brother had not done this crime, but there was so much political pressure around the case that they had to find and convict a perpetrator. He fit the profile, and so he was found guilty and sentenced to death. Turns out he hadn't even been at the scene, but he could not get a retrial. This happens more often than you would think.

So, why couldn't we adopt this model of fellowship and comradery for death-row inmates across the country, and let them commune with other men on the row? Obviously, mental health and safety are the top priority, but I've seen it work powerfully. Why can't we treat these men like humans before we take their life? In my opinion, prisons don't even try this method because the inmates aren't worth it in the eyes of the state, or they are afraid of outcomes that they haven't measured, tested, or even studied before. It would take nothing more than a space for them to meet and an officer to oversee it. And the truth is, there is rarely, if any, violence on the row because all these men have the same fate, the same destination, and are facing the same end. Human isolation is the worst form of punishment, and we desperately need human connection. This practice of daily or weekly fellowship brings them together, and they are more compassionate with one another than inmates in the general population. These hated men changed my life forever, and I mourn whenever yet another of my brothers is taken from this world.

On the Row at Angola

I've had the privilege of serving at Angola State Prison in Louisiana several times. We stayed for the weekend three different times and actually slept in death-row cells. This is the old building that housed death-row inmates for years before they built new housing for those residents who are destined to die at the hands of the state. It's hard to describe the feeling of sleeping in that tiny cell on that hard mat and rubber pillow, and showering in an open room where the water is cold and comes out so strong it stings the skin. Having to wait for the doors to open so we could go to breakfast was surreal, and it's something I will never forget. I've even been strapped to the gurney where they carry out the executions just so I could experience what that feels like.

For decades, Angola State Prison was known as "the bloodiest prison in the world." It sits on eighteen thousand acres in rural Louisiana and is bordered on three sides by the Mississippi River. The land was once a huge plantation, and the prison still produces corn, soy, green beans, catfish, cattle, and other goods sold on the open market. They have an entire kennel of dozens of bloodhounds that would easily find you if you escaped, if the land didn't get you before they rounded you up. There are over six thousand inmates residing there, which makes it the largest prison in the country. Over five thousand of those men are doing life without the possibility of parole. In Louisiana, a life sentence means natural life with no chance of ever going home. A life sentence typically has an end date when an offender is eligible for parole, but not in this case. The inmates call that sentence "all day long," and they even have a graveyard where inmates who have no family are buried. They also have a beautiful program where inmates provide hospice care for their dying brothers, since they have no one who can give them that love before they pass. There are nine freestanding churches on the property, and inmates who have completed ministry degrees can actually become pastors and lead those churches. I've seen it with my own eyes, otherwise I wouldn't have believed it.

On one of my visits, as we went from cell to cell on death row looking through the bars, there were three basic reactions from the residents: Some lay on the bunks with their backs to us, meaning they weren't interested. Others were eager to come to us, as they were starved for human interaction. Some, however, watched from a distance, not knowing why we were there or what we wanted. That was the posture of one of the young men I stood in front of that day. He looked at me like he wasn't sure if he wanted to talk. I said, "As-salamu alaikum," as I noticed his Quran sitting on his bedside table. He returned the greeting and came toward me. When I reached my hand through the bars, he shook it and saw one of my tattoos.

He noticed the Arabic writing for peace, which is salaam, and asked me why I had that on my arm. I told him I came in peace and it was for him. He said, "Why are you here?" to which I replied, "Because I love you, brother."

He responded, "How can you love me? You don't even know me."

I said, "If I was on the other side of those bars, and you were over here, I know I would want someone to tell me that."

He replied, "So, you love me? Well, *your* book says if you love a brother, you should be willing to give your life for him. Would you die for me, brother?"

I paused. "I'd like to think I would, but I'm not sure if I'm that good of a man. But I hope I would."

He smiled. "That's what's up. Honesty." Then he looked into my eyes. "Would you come back to see me?" I told him I would try, and we shook hands again, this time with more compassion, before saying goodbye.

In a matter of a few minutes, two men with seemingly nothing in common made a deep connection. He was about half my age, and happened to be black, Muslim, and sitting on death row. We shared nothing in common on the outside, but inside was a whole different story. If we stop and look for similarities rather than all the differences we have, we will find that our journeys are more similar than we realize. This was a beautiful interaction between two men on separate journeys crossing paths, and connected by a tattoo and some real dialogue.

Let's move on. In the final act, we will discuss the battle raging for the hearts and minds of our kids. We will also profile an iconic, but forgotten, civil-rights city, and their reemergence as a model for the nation.

Act Four

MODERN-DAY HEROES

Jeff Wadstrom and Coach Ulises with the Boys of Tijuana

During my time in Tijuana, I witnessed things that impacted me so profoundly that I wrote a book called *Protect the Dream* to help student-athletes based on what I learned there. I met a soccer coach through my friend Jeff Wadstrom. Ulises Romero was a professional soccer player in Mexico before he found his life's passion in Tijuana. He helps change kids' lives by getting them off the streets, away from gangs, and back in school. His soccer club, Letics Sports, is a safe haven for kids who are in great danger. Young boys and girls are kidnapped off the streets in Tijuana at alarming rates. Ulises takes them in, giving many of them a place to live, and helps them become great soccer players, but more importantly, better young men and women. I played soccer from age six all the way into college and had many coaches, and he is the most effective coach I've ever seen. A number of his kids have signed professional contracts themselves, and pro teams have begun to scout their players in Tijuana because of his success. However, he teaches them much more than just soccer. They learn to look out for one another, protect one another, dream big dreams, and love more starving kids into the club. They recently launched a program where they're feeding hundreds of families in their poor community in the middle of a global pandemic.

Coach Ulises and his Letics Club are making a significant impact in Tijuana with very little financial support. I can only imagine what they could do with resources. Currently they need a home big enough to house the players he is rescuing from the streets, and Bridge to the Future Foundation in San Diego is working to make that dream a reality.

I cannot even imagine taking thirty kids into a small home in one of the most dangerous cities in the world. I long to have that kind of selfless, courageous, sacrificial heart. Ulises is a much better man than me, and he reminds me that there are many unlikely heroes out there in some of the most unexpected places.

Young Role Models

There's an army of invisible heroes out there putting their lives on the line to save others. They are unseen, and they're operating on fields in areas of the world most of us would never go to. I've met so many men and women along this fascinating journey who have changed my life by their example and their devotion to the least of us. However, when I witness young people laying down their lives to rescue others from darkness, it gives me hope for a young generation who are losing their way.

Billy Ponchito (far left) and His Letics Teammates

Billy's Courage

One of the kids Ulises rescued was a young man named Billy. When I first met him, he stood out as one of the most joyful kids on the team. He always had a smile on his face, and he was the first to show up and the last to leave. While being a good player, he wasn't the best, but he was by far the greatest servant and helper to Ulises. Sometimes the other players made fun of him because he was so happy and always so willing to help his team.

One day Billy was waiting at a taxi stand while on his way home from practice. Suddenly, a car screeched to a halt across the street and two men got out of the vehicle. This stretch of road often has bodies dumped nearby, and there are lots of kidnappings and murders by Sicarios. Sicarios are the ones the cartels send to collect debts, hurt people, and if need be, eliminate those who don't pay or who cross the cartel.

A young lady with her baby was standing by the road as the two men approached her. They were going to kidnap the baby and sell it on the black market. That is hard for me to write, as I believe it is one of the most heinous crimes imaginable. Babies now are the most lucrative "product," as the buyer can raise the child into whatever they want them to be.

Billy didn't hesitate as he ran toward the scene. He managed to get between the mother and the would-be kidnappers, and he shielded them as she struggled to get away. Billy was executed on the spot, and his body was dumped three miles away. He gave his life willingly to save another, which is the highest expression of love. The mother and her baby had to flee to another city and can never return to Tijuana. Billy's family also had to leave town, never to return. I wonder what I would have done in the same situation. Would I have frozen? Would I have counted the cost before making a move? I would have been too late. I hope I could be like Billy and put another's needs and safety above my own. But I will never know, because I've never faced such a situation.

Billy has become the standard for what we are teaching these kids to be. We created a special POPP award in his honor: the Billy Ponchito Courage Award, only given to kids who exemplify tremendous courage in the service of others. There are heroes south of the border, even if you never see them on the news.

A Young Man's Fall

One of Billy's teammates was a boy we'll call Juan. I know him to this day. He's a good player, but he has a different temperament than Billy. A little tougher, Juan has a reputation as a good fighter. Whenever his team would get into a scrap, he was a good player to have around. Juan's father is a strong man who has connections to the dark world in Tijuana. I met him on one of my trips down there, and I was able to interview him about his time at La Mesa prison, where I had run my Forty Days to Freedom program earlier that year. He has a fascinating story, and I was impressed with his strength and how he wanted so much better for his son.

One day Juan began to drift from his teammates. Eventually he moved to another town about an hour from Tijuana, where he started running with a different crowd, and before long he was selling drugs. Being strong, tough, and talented served him well, and eventually he had his own crew. The job he was working with his mother paid him two dollars a day, whereas this new hustle paid him six hundred dollars a week. That's hard to say no to for a kid from the streets. The next time I saw him it looked like his eyes had died. I remembered the playful kid I had gotten to know and the joy he had playing with his teammates and following Ulises. It broke my heart.

Finally Juan came to his senses and reached out to his coach, the one man he could trust. Ulises is now trying to help this young man change his life. Most don't get a second chance in that dark world, and we hope Juan makes the most of it. Perhaps he can learn from Billy and be a light to kids who are running toward the darkness and help them see where that road leads. Juan had someone to reach out to on his darkest day. Sadly, many of today's youth only have the streets, and those streets have an expiration date. We need more men like Ulises to show them a better way.

Chapter Thirteen
VIOLENCE AND A YOUNG GENERATION

Young people today are at terrible risk of being thrown into the correctional system, whether they live in our inner cities or the suburbs. Consider the world they inherited from us.

Today, kids want things too quick and easy. They are the drive-through generation. Kids can get answers quickly on Google and YouTube, and they can get what they want delivered the same day on Amazon. They can stream movies and videos, and have a million songs in their pocket. If they don't record it and post it, it didn't happen. They can get a no-strings-attached date for the night by simply "swiping right." They have every nasty video ever produced in their pocket, and now they're having a hard time in their relationships because they've been raised on high-speed internet porn. They are a wartime generation, as America has been at war their whole lives, making them the first generation to have lived with war for this long. Violence and conflict have become second nature to them, even if only subconsciously.

They're the first of their kind in our nation. They are a pill generation who grew up watching commercials that taught them there is a medical answer for every emotion. Suicide and overdose are a normal part of their lives with their friends, and it doesn't shock them anymore. They are an experiment. They are the generation who all got participation trophies and couldn't play dodgeball because we told them they might get hurt. They are the ones we rescued from trouble and whose side we took against the school when educators disciplined them for poor behavior. We have produced a generation of young men and women who often give up when they hit their first big failure in their twenties and consider ending it all like many of their friends have. They aren't allowed to fail, and we push them to get straight A's, go to the right college, and pick a sport or extracurricular to excel at. They are a terribly stressed-out and depressed generation. What went wrong?

They are judged by how many friends, views, likes, shares, followers, and subscribers they have. There are certain body types they believe they must have in order to be popular, and they'll do almost anything to get there. Girls are pressured to lose their virginity in high school, and are ridiculed and bullied if they don't. Pills are sold and passed around the hallways and classrooms. Are you stressed? Xanax. Need to pull an all-nighter? Adderall. Feel a little blue? Celexa. Can't sleep? Ambien. Feeling some pain? Vicodin. If you don't like how you feel, there's a pharmaceutical solution. When we depend on chemicals to medicate our moods, we cease to grow emotionally, as we don't experience anger, happiness, sadness, or fear; we simply mask it and dull it out.

This generation has grown up glorifying violence. Their music is gangster rap, and they pump an average of fifty to a hundred songs a day straight into their ears through their Beats or EarPods. They master video games like *Grand Theft Auto* and *Call of Duty*, where they get to experience virtual killing. They watch movies like *The Purge*, where crime and violence are cool and even recommended. Their social media gives them a steady dose of sex, drugs, and rock 'n 'roll, where everyone can be a model, pop star, comedian, or actor, all without leaving their bedroom. They have made bullying an art form, and they can destroy someone anonymously with a keystroke, with no real consequences—except for the harm their victim will often do to themselves.

They get their news from social media and word of mouth, and they have lost connection with their parents' generation because they don't believe they need them anymore. Every great culture teaches the young their history through stories, songs, and legends as they pass on the wisdom of their ancestors. These young people get their knowledge through Google, Instagram, and YouTube. They most likely don't know anything about their own family line beyond their grandparents. So, where is the next King, Gandhi, or Mandela? What about the next young Maya Angelou, Mother Teresa, or Harriet Tubman? It's time to find them and introduce them to their true selves.

Old Heads

Tough kids today call us grown folks "old heads." They learned a different code on the streets, because many of the strong, influential men in their neighborhoods are doing time and living by the convict code. They think we have no clue about their world. With no one to teach them, they simply changed the rules. With the older convicts, doing time was more honorable and they handled conflict the old-fashioned way: man to man, one on one, with hands, in the shower. After it's over, it's over; the beef is squashed.

The "Nineties Babies" got more efficient. They are called that because they were born after 1990. They figured three on one with knives made more sense and got more done more quickly. They did away with the honor code. They attack for no reason but envy and greed, while the old guys had to get permission to smash on a guy or else suffer the consequences. So, the old guys on the inside have washed their hands of the young ones, believing they are beyond redemption. The generational divide is growing wider than ever, even more so than with earlier generations. One big reason is that these young ones have had access to technology their whole lives, while the old heads have never had it, or never for very long, depending on how long they've been behind the wire.

We challenge and expect the older men to mentor the young ones, and the young brothers to respect their elders. It's not easy, but with conversation and each side working the steps, they begin to respect one another and bridge the divide. I've seen this model work time and time again in some of the toughest prisons in the country. There is no way we can reform a broken system if we don't train the wiser men to teach the younger men and break the cycle of violence they're learning on the streets. Young people need mentors, and if they don't have any, they will simply create their own ways of dealing with life.

Young and Wild

There's a whole generation growing up without strong men involved in their lives. They are the kids who were born to the women whose men are in the system, or those who were born to young, single mothers in poor communities where many of the strong men are missing. We've lost a whole generation of strong men through the war on crime, and they are now rotting away on the chain gang.

The convict code has clearly defined rules of conduct and predictable outcomes for violations. But the young man's code has few rules and is anything but predictable. These young people have figured out the quickest and easiest ways to get what they want. They haven't been accountable to the streets like their fathers' generation was. So, they make their own rules and dish out their own justice as they see fit.

The old heads say these kids have no code, no honor. They say they're a waste of time, that these young men are more like animals and have no respect. But I am quick to point out that they would have a proper code if the older brothers and fathers had stayed in the free world to teach them instead of abandoning their sons, little brothers, grandsons, and nephews. It makes them mad when I say that, but then they realize it's true. I challenge them to become the heroes this young generation desperately needs, and many of them are answering the call.

Generation Z and the 2020 Protests

When the protests began in the spring of 2020, it created the perfect storm. Today's young people—or Generation Z, as they are being labeled—have been preparing for this time, unknowingly, and we've been helping them. They've been practicing on their devices, their screens, and their many apps. However, this time it wasn't a movie or a rap video or a video game. This was live and in person, up close and personal.

Do you think they were going to miss it? This is the coolest thing many of them have ever seen and it is real, not virtual. Their phones are in the air during these protests and they are posting, sharing, and tweeting like never before. The one who shoots the most shocking or dangerous video gets the most cred. The protests have become a grand reality show for them. The pandemic provides masks so they can be anonymous, if need be, and the masks can also be a political statement or a fashion show, even if they don't know much about the cause or the issues at hand. When asked what they are protesting for, typically they share a sound bite, something they saw on Instagram, their primary news platform. Whatever is trending and cool is what gets the most airplay in their world.

This is the first time a revolution of this scale has been on twenty-four-hour media for everyone to see. And when the protests became violent, as the rioters and looters seized the moment, that made for awesome video content. When young people get closer and closer to the real violence, not merely on a screen, the temptation is sometimes too much to bear. One picks up a bottle and throws it, and it gets dropped on Instagram or Snapchat. Another taunts the police and it gets airplay, and cool points skyrocket. They have finally found their movement, and they feel as if they finally have a voice. They've been wanting to say something significant for quite some time; they just didn't have anything to say. However, all this drama is having serious consequences on the young mind.

The Treacherous Twenties

Many of you have probably heard of the infamous "Twenty-Seven Club." It's a list composed mostly of musicians, artists, and actors who died at the young age of twenty-seven. Notable members include Janis Joplin, Jimi Hendrix, Jim Morrison, Kurt Cobain, and Amy Winehouse. There is something dangerous about that particular stretch of life in the midtwenties. I often wondered if it was some coincidental phenomenon, or if there was something really going on behind the scenes that we have been unaware of.

Today we are witnessing an alarming and growing epidemic among our youth. Kids are moving into their twenties and experiencing real depression, anxiety, internal rage, and a very real feeling of hopelessness. It is the perfect storm. They have been babysat by screens, and sheltered and protected from failure and consequences. Many have been medicated since they were young. They are experiencing more and more pressure to fit in and to become what everyone wants them to be, and they're left comparing their insides to everyone else's outsides. When they don't measure up, they reach for something. Drugs are an easy option—all you have to do is ask a friend and they will know who can get you what you need. Almost half of young people who develop a prescription-drug habit got their first pills from their parents' medicine cabinet or a friend's parents. We are a medicated society, and our children are watching, learning, and now stealing our medication.

Anger, fear, sadness, and anxiety are normal emotions for a teenager. Generations before us either learned how to cope or they didn't, but medication was rarely the treatment. Nowadays when kids feel the first signs of sadness, lethargy, or distraction, their parents take them to their family doctor and ask for a remedy. That's what we have taught them. So, when they begin experiencing real pain, why are they going to listen to us when we say "don't do drugs"? They have more avenues for unhealthy escape than we did back in the day. When they want to change how they feel, they can go to social media for distraction, music for background noise, gaming for escape, or movies for entertainment. However, all that does is bury the emotions deeper and postpone the meltdown. These kids have made escaping, avoiding, and denying an art form, but they learned it from us. We created the things they are using to soothe and medicate, but we failed to teach them how to use these tools responsibly.

They go into young adulthood not having had many significant victories over failure, defeat, or tough challenges. Instead, they have run from the things that make them feel bad and have developed unhealthy coping mechanisms. Kids are more and more closed off to their parents, and have become sophisticated liars to avoid consequences. It is rare to find young people who are comfortable talking about what is really hurting them inside, so they are left to suffer alone, though surrounded by so many. Previous generations had more interaction with their parents around the dinner table or by spending quality time together, before technology took most of that away. If you are not accustomed to spending meaningful time with your parents, why would you trust them with your deepest pain or biggest secrets?

Here's where it gets even more dangerous. Most of these kids have friends they have lost, or at least have friends of friends who have passed. Every high school, and even some middle schools, must prepare to deal with kids hurting themselves or others, and dying from accidental overdoses or from self-harm. When I ask kids to raise their hands if they have lost any friends to overdose or suicide, tragically, almost every hand in the room goes up. And every time we lose another one, social media blows up with sympathy and sadness, and the soul we've lost has a short time of fame among their peers. Everybody blasts it on their media, because their friends will, and they'll seem heartless if they don't share about losing a "friend." Sadly, many of the kids pouring out their sorrow didn't even know the kid or hang out with them, but when they attend the memorial it's as if they were best friends. Our kids are being desensitized to death, and when things go dark for them, they have that option in the back of their mind. If they're honest, most kids today will tell you they have definitely considered suicide. I went through a number of tough things and some dark times as a teen, but suicide never entered my mind as an option or solution.

When they get out of college or out of their parents' homes, they are no longer surrounded by friends or classmates like they have been for the past fifteen years since grade school. Now they are in this place called "the real world" that they have feared for quite some time. Many have a whole new friend set, and the pattern of trying to fit in and keep up repeats. They are comparing their real-world lives with the lives they think their high school and college friends are living on social media, even though most of those kids are feeling the same way. This is a cocktail for disaster. When that first job is lost, or the love of their life leaves, or they get arrested for the first time, they go to that dark place. Alcohol and drug use escalates, or they begin acting out in unhealthy ways. When the stress, anxiety, and depression get too intense, they consider an easier way out, a way to be truly loved and for the pain to stop. Tragically, we now have another member of the "Twenty-Seven Club."

Medicating Youth Pain

We are seeing an epidemic rise in opioid use, especially among our youth, because our kids are in pain. They are being squeezed, stretched, and suffocated, and their psychological pain is becoming unbearable. I remember my first surgery as a young athlete, one of twelve I would go on to have. From the first time my doctor prescribed painkillers, I really enjoyed them. They took the edge off and removed my uneasiness and anxiety. For a few hours I felt comfortable. But it wasn't the physical pain I was medicating; it was the psychological suffering. That's why I understand these kids, because I've been there. But the game has changed. Recently I heard of a girl who got her wisdom teeth out. The doctor prescribed thirty Vicodin and also thirty Percocet, just in case. That's criminal. All we got was a frozen bag of peas to put on our swollen cheeks. If this girl wanted to, she could now share those pills with her friends or sell them at school. This is a very real scenario.

Imagine a party where kids are passing around painkillers to party with, Adderall to study with, Xanax to take the edge off, and alcohol and weed as a baseline. And here's a new trend that will keep parents up at night: Boys secretly put a Xanax or two in a girl's drink, and she won't remember anything the next day. It's tragic that we have to train our teenage daughters not to leave their drink unattended and to keep their hand over their cup just in case. But now it's getting even worse as drug dealers get smarter and more deliberate—welcome to the terrifying drug fentanyl. We've never seen anything like it.

Fentanyl was created to help people die. That's it. It's the super-painkiller that is given to hospice patients to make them comfortable so they can pass without unbearable pain. Huge quantities are smuggled into Mexico from China, and then it moves through the tunnels across the borders and on to major cities across the United States. It's so powerful that those who chop it up and cut it have to wear masks and gloves, because if you touch it or breathe it, it can be lethal.

This drug is fifty to one hundred times more potent than heroin, and it is hitting the streets where your kids live. The cartels and street gangs figured out that if they add just a little fentanyl to the heroin—and now to cocaine as well—the demand skyrockets. They continue adding a little at a time until junkies start dying on the streets. That's all they need. Once word gets out there's a new package in town that's killing junkies, everybody wants it, even kids from the suburbs. Did you catch that? Drug addicts are chasing the batch that is killing people on the streets, because it will take them to a higher place free from anxiety, depression, and pain. Nobody believes it will get them too; they believe they're smarter than the streets. Until they're not.

If we don't find a way to reach our kids and help them unpack and unravel what is hurting them, then we are going to continue losing more and more. The only answer I see is mentoring, and we need people who understand their pain from experience. Typically, kids will only listen to an old head if they believe we have walked in their shoes and felt their pain.

The Wisdom of Sir Brown

Male prisons are basically the streets without females. A lot that goes on in the free world is the same behind these walls. Here's my attitude: Prison should be a place to rebuild or renew yourself to create a better you. You're overweight? There is time and people who can help you sculpt a new body. Struggling with reading? There are guys who can assist you with that. You want to get a better understanding of the God of your choosing? Guys are in place to help you along with that too. I mean amazing athletic trainers, teacher's aides, Islamic and biblical scholars that will blow your mind. But energy isn't neutral. There's positive and negative. And you have not experienced true evil until you've entered some of these facilities. You like violence? You've come to the right place. People are on edge. Forgotten, unloved, and uncared for. They're bitter and seek anyone they can take their frustrations out on.

God help you if you walk into one of these dorms with a major drug addiction. I would say the majority of guys behind these walls have some form of vice—tobacco, alcohol, or even harder drugs. I have no idea how drugs get into an institution, and I would never ask. That's not my business. But the aftereffects are obvious to anyone with eyes. What may cost ten dollars on the street costs a hundred or more here. If you receive any of this stuff on credit, God be with you if you can't pay on time. And once you miss a payment, interest is added, or else you will receive a decent amount of pain for being delinquent.

Just like the streets, junkies demean and embarrass themselves. They stop bathing and grooming, and forget about their personal appearance. They smell, and they get kicked out of cells and cell blocks. And worst of all, some lose their lives or become snitches. Being a snitch can appear attractive to a new inmate. They get promised things and compensated for information. But that life is always short-lived. This world is too small. Someone will find out, and it's guaranteed the snitching was not worth it. Plus, even the person you are snitching to doesn't respect a snitch.

Addiction behind these walls is a lose-lose situation. There is never enough to satisfy your habit for long. The expense drains family members and resources. Plus, there are severe penalties for failing a urinalysis test: hole time, loss of visitation privileges, loss of eligibility for parole or halfway house, or even loss of the ability to purchase commissary. The drug game is ugly in the free world, but behind these walls, it resembles Medusa.

Chapter Fourteen
YOUNG MEN NEED STRONG MEN

It seems the older I get, the more I'm scratching my head with today's youth. I spend time with them all the time, and I observe. I catch myself saying more and more often, "That kid just wasn't raised right." Common courtesy is rare with these teens, disrespect of authorities is rampant, and objectification of the opposite sex is out of control. We can't just blame everything on technology and social media; that's lazy. Something bigger is missing, and we need to figure this young generation out before it's too late. Young people today, especially young men, lack strong male role models. Period. Young men need strong men, and there is no other way around it.

The Natural Order of Things

In ancient cultures, young men were raised by elders who taught them responsibility, character, rites of passage, and how to support and protect their families and loved ones. Traditions were passed along, and wisdom was handed down as families spent quality time together and spoke about the things that really matter. Those valuable traditions appear to have become a lost art, at least in the West. Technology has replaced meaningful connection, and for the most part, this young generation has been neglected, forcing them to come up with their own ideas about life. We have robbed them of the skills they will desperately need as they grow into young men, start families, and raise sons of their own. Nothing can replace the spoken word and the human connection young people need to develop into responsible, productive, and healthy members of society. We have taken shortcuts, and our sons and grandsons are paying the price for our shortcomings.

If I had to pick one issue plaguing our society in regard to crime and violence, it would be the absent father. When I say absent father, you might immediately think of kids in poor minority communities, but this problem is not confined to any particular demographic. A father can be absent while still in the house. I believe every boy or girl, on some level, has daddy issues, whether it be that their father was never involved in their life or he just wasn't very nice. Sometimes they're domineering, suffocating, or exasperating. Or, it could be that they're seemingly perfect, and the son or daughter never believes they can measure up. Some kids have been hurt by their dads, while others have been neglected. Either way, we all carry wounds from our fathers.

Young men need strong men, and if they don't have them, they will gravitate toward anyone else who is paying them attention. Boys and girls who are not being validated by their fathers will look for it in other places. Some turn to coaches or pastors, some turn to older guys who impress them, and some tragically turn to the gangs. As parents, it can be terrifying to face this truth, but predators are on the lookout for wounded young souls who are desperate to find a place to belong. It could be a young lady who is talking to men online, or a boy who has found a trusted older friend who happens to be a youth minister who pays him extra attention after church. Our kids are in great danger in today's world because many of them lack the self-worth and self-esteem that come from a healthy relationship with strong men who truly care about their well-being. I recently asked a group of high school kids about the subject of "sugar daddies" that I kept hearing about. Was it real? They all laughed and shook their heads like, *Yes, this is real with teens today.* Sugar daddies are older men who will take care of a young girl financially in return for sex. This is more common than you would believe, even at your local high school. Many kids today don't even think it's a big deal.

Early in my daughter's life, I was given some great advice from a mentor. He said, "You need to 'date' your daughter so she knows how a young man is supposed to treat her." I chose Thursdays as the day for our weekly Daddy Date. Each week we would go to lunch, or a movie, or just go to the mall together. She would hold my hand in the mall even after she was in high school. We stopped when I started getting funny looks! I did my best to model for her how a man is supposed to treat her, so that when some young knucklehead treats her disrespectfully, she will immediately know something isn't right.

If a young woman has no relationship with her father, she will be desperate to find someone, anyone, who will pay her attention and make her feel beautiful and safe. They are vulnerable in a world full of men looking for wounded young women. Just look at Instagram today and you'll see countless young women using their bodies to get attention from young men. But older men are watching too, and even masquerading as teens. All they have to do is create a new profile and speak their language. Maybe we haven't taught our daughters about the threats, or worse, we haven't learned about them for ourselves. It's tragic and so preventable. If a father doesn't have the time to pour into his kids, then he is just too busy. We can never get that time with them back, time when they are so impressionable and need someone to tell them everything is going to be all right.

Grandfathers Are the Pillars

Young people today are becoming more and more disconnected from their past. I wonder how many really know their grandfathers, their stories, and their life journeys. If we don't know where we come from, we will miss valuable life lessons we were intended to receive. Now that I am a grandfather, I feel so responsible to be a big part of my grandsons' lives. I feel as though it is my responsibility to teach them what I know and be another voice in addition to their father, who happens to be a great dad. We need a host of strong, spiritual men around our sons and daughters if we are going to change this world. The next generation is the key, but we have to reach them.

My grandfather is the greatest man I've ever known. He was a captain in the Navy and an aircraft-carrier pilot. My mom grew up on Navy bases and met my dad when they were stationed in Maryland. My dad was the lifeguard at the pool, and she started seeing him on the down low, as captains' daughters weren't allowed to date enlisted men!

My Pop-Pop, Carl Greene Tiedemann, was a direct descendant of General Nathanael Greene, who was one of General Washington's righthand men during the Revolutionary War. Washington sent General Greene to the South to drive out Cornwallace, which he did, and that proved to be a turning point in the war. As a reward for his service, soon-to-be President Washington gave Greene a large portion of Savannah, and he was laid to rest beneath a big monument there in Johnson Square. Nathanael Greene has a statue in the Hall of Heroes inside the US Capitol Building in Washington, DC, and it made me so proud when I saw it for myself.

My grandfather never had to raise his voice, and I never saw him lose his temper. He never wasted his words, so when he did speak, everyone listened. He never demanded respect; it was simply given. He carried himself in a way that made everyone feel safe and secure when he was around. I only remember one time when I disrespected him, and it was by accident. I was about fifteen years old, and he let me know it was wrong. I never forgot it, nor did I ever make the same mistake again. He didn't raise his voice, nor did he have to say it twice. I just wanted to do well for him, not because he demanded it, but because I didn't want to disappoint him. He made me want to be a better kid.

Pop-Pop rarely drank, didn't smoke, and never used foul language. He treated my grandmother like a queen, and she didn't have to work for a living. She was an extraordinary homemaker, which is very valuable work, in my opinion. He believed it was the man's job to support his family. He bought a ranch in Flagstaff, Arizona, and was one of the hardest-working men I've ever known. He always did his work excellently. He was honest and always treated people fairly. He built the church where his family worshipped, but I rarely heard him discuss his faith; he just lived it. I've always wondered what kind of man I would be if he had raised me. I'll never know, but I firmly believe I would be a better man by far.

Years after he died, I developed a process that helped me to do things much more excellently, and it still serves me today. Many of the things I listed above about my granddad happen to be shortcomings for me, and things I still have to work on regularly. So, I began asking myself when doing a chore or an assignment, "What would Pop-Pop do?" Invariably I start over, or correct my work, or finish something I am about to procrastinate on. Decades after his death, he is still impacting my life, and I pray that somewhere up there he is proud of me and the man he helped me become.

What young people need now more than ever are men of integrity watching over their lives. It is the natural order of things. Human beings were not designed to be raised by technology or merely learn things from YouTube. Those are fine as complementary tools, but in no way do they replace a father, grandfather, or uncle who is supposed to pass on the wisdom of their elders to the next generation. I miss my Pop-Pop, and I hope I can be a positive role model to young men who need a good example of what a real man looks like.

Walking through Hell with My Son

The world changed on March 12, 2020. The pandemic, followed by an economic collapse and then protests in the streets, provided a firestorm. Little did I know that one of the most important battles of my life was about to begin. We don't choose these storms; we just pray we are prepared when they come. Mine would come through my son, who was about to turn twenty-five. The midtwenties are proving to be treacherous waters these days for young Millennials. Their brilliance, awareness, and mastery over technology has provided them advantages, but it also comes with unique mental, emotional, and spiritual challenges.

My son is very much like me, but he also possesses talents and skills that I do not. He is social and charismatic, but also driven and hard on himself. He sailed through high school with straight A's, graduating with honors. Then he sailed through college at the University of Georgia with straight A's, and graduated summa cum laude. Things have always come relatively easy for him, just like they did for me. He landed a great job, even before he graduated, as the director of marketing for a small software company. Everything was going as planned, and then the storm came.

Those who have never dealt with depression have a hard time

understanding those who are dealing with it. It isn't simply feeling a little down or a little blue, and it's not something you can just "snap out of." I counseled people in ministry for years without really understanding it, until it hit me in 2002. It was debilitating and exhausting. It was one of the toughest battles I have ever fought. But this was different, because now it was visiting my son for the first time. Nothing precipitated it, and it was not circumstantial; it just showed up. I call it the "Black Dog," as Winston Churchill called his. Luckily, I had walked through that storm before, and I was prepared to walk through it with my boy.

It's a whole different kind of pain when our children suffer. It goes deeper than our own, and we would trade places with them in a second if we could just carry their burden for them. That is true selfless, sacrificial love that we can only experience when our loved ones suffer. This one tore me apart. I was afraid like I had never been, and I carried it constantly and never put it down. There was no way to avoid it or deny it; I had to accept it and deal with it. I can't imagine what would have happened if we hadn't forged the relationship, father and son, that we would need to make it through this darkness.

Right before the quarantine is when the Black Dog arrived for him. He would have to go through this alone, but on the phone with me every day. To complicate things further, a sleep disorder set in, and he went with little to no sleep for the next three months. Do you know how it feels when you have a night with no sleep? Imagine a few nights. We begin to feel like zombies. Thoughts and words don't come easy, and motivation is nonexistent. Now imagine ninety days and ninety sleepless nights. Some who are reading this have been there too, but many won't talk about it because of the stigma and shame that accompanies mental-health issues. That needs to change.

I am so grateful he was open with me, as I know many father/son relationships where real communication about important issues is rare, until there is a crisis. It's hard to establish trust and vulnerability in the midst of a violent storm. Those must be developed during "peace time" so you are ready when the bullets start flying. We had been cultivating this relationship for years, unlike my father and me. My dad tried to be there for me, but we didn't have a foundation that allowed me to feel comfortable sharing my greatest fears and deepest pain with him. So, I kept it to myself. I'm sure we both wanted it, but we didn't know how to get there together. When my storms came as a young man, I walked through them alone and kept my secrets.

My son and I talked on the phone every single day for three months, sometimes multiple times a day, if needed. Most times he didn't want to talk, but we talked anyway. I would send him texts of encouragement and inspiration, and we formulated strategies and battle plans together, and established healthy daily routines that we held each other accountable to. He gave me permission to do that. We engaged a therapist, a sleep-disorder specialist, and we tried medications to help him through the toughest parts with the help of our primary physician. We tackled his diet, as well as his exercise routine, which was challenging with insomnia, depression, and anxiety. We installed a spiritual component that consisted of music, meditation, and cognitive behavioral therapy. We came up with mantras together, we cried together, and we made pledges to one another. We had victories and setbacks. Each time, we had to get back up together and recommit, not knowing if the end was in sight or if things would ever return to some sort of normalcy.

In this battle for the hearts and minds of our kids, there are no easy fixes and no shortcuts. I believe too many parents these days are looking for others to fix their problems, whether it be through therapy, counseling, or medication, and although they care deeply, they are not necessarily walking through it with their child. These kids feel all alone. They feel as if their friends aren't there, their parents don't understand, and the noise in their heads is overwhelming. There is no easy solution, and one size definitely does not fit all.

This story has a happy ending. My son not only came out of the darkness, but he is wiser, more determined, and deeper today than he's ever been. He is just as talented, driven, and gregarious, but much more self-aware. This trial by fire made him stronger and brought us closer together than we had ever been. He recently sent me a text that meant the world to me: "I went into a deep darkness, Dad, but now I'm the smartest, strongest, and most confident person I've ever been. Thanks for raising me the way that you did, and thank you for sticking with me through it all, Pops. I love you more than you'll ever know." That's all a father ever dreams of hearing from his son. I couldn't be prouder of him.

Bridging the Divide between Cops and Kids

When everything blew up after the George Floyd killing, the call was for community conversations. These are crucial for bridging the divide that is growing wider and wider between our youth and our law enforcement. The key is productive dialogue and compassionate communication. We must try to understand one another. However, what I witnessed, while well-meaning, were awkward attempts at discussions and uncomfortable silence in between comments. It wasn't that people didn't want to talk, but more that they didn't know where to begin or what to say. One side is afraid to be honest for fear of negative consequences, while the other side fears speaking up because they're being told they don't have the right to share on these issues because they cannot truly understand. What is left by the end of the conversation is frustration and discouragement. Some of those events are doing more harm than good, in my opinion. It's even harder to discuss these things with young people, so we need to get creative.

We need to get the conversation going in a way that empowers people to discuss solutions, and to understand what the other side is feeling. So, a detective friend of mine, Zach Bihari, came up with an idea. We engaged the support of two of our police chiefs outside of Atlanta. Chief Wayne Dennard and Chief Bill Westenberger are two of the finest men I know, and they are outstanding examples of how police officers should serve and protect our communities. Part of our high school program involves bringing in officers to share about their lives, so we can show the kids there is a heart behind the badge. We decided to build on that, but take it a step further. So, we are launching a new program. Utilizing the training facility at one of the police precincts, the kids will go through an actual training module taught by police instructors. For one hour they learn some of what the officers experience in their use-of-force training. With all that young people are hearing these days about police tactics and brutality, we thought it would be constructive for them to see precisely what the officers are learning.

But here's where it gets fun. Having completed the training module, next they go into the virtual simulator and put what they just learned into practice. They put on the virtual goggles and get a revolver that looks like a real gun, weighs the same, and even recoils similar to a real pistol, but it doesn't shoot anything but lasers. The kids will have to make snap decisions in real time and decide if and when to use force, and when to shoot or not shoot based on the threat level.

Sometimes they will choose right, and sometimes they will fail. If nothing else, this will be an experience they will never forget, like a video game on steroids with the very latest technology. Afterward, we serve a meal and they discuss how they did, what they felt, and what they learned. Then the officers share about the challenges they face on a daily basis. This opens the door for kids to share about how they feel when pulled over, or find themselves in other, similar circumstances. We create healthy dialogue as the officers learn more about how kids feel during these troubling times, and the teens walk a mile in the officers' shoes before they judge them. The teens learn to see the men and women in blue differently, and the officers begin to see this young generation through a different lens as well. This is just one idea, and there are many more that can help bridge the growing divide between cops and kids.

Unless we get very intentional, things will continue to unravel with our kids during these confusing times. They are seeing disrespect of authorities in every area of their lives, and they are imitating what we model for them. How can we expect them to respect authorities when they see political candidates ridiculing one another on TV? Much less when they see young people taunting police in the streets with no consequences. Now is the time we need to rally around these kids. Before it's too late.

Chapter Fifteen
REGARDING WHITE PRIVILEGE

I feel compelled to share this next, in the same way I feel obligated to tell the brothers behind the wire that on some level, I understand why I might be here and they might be there. They love to hear these stories and to see a brother of less color who might just *get it*. I know this is a controversial subject, so please bear with me and withhold judgment. I do not expect anyone to share my conviction on this issue—that's up to you. But this is my story.

I was born into a white, conservative family in Marietta, Georgia, just outside of Atlanta and right smack in the middle of the Bible Belt. We were middle class, and at the school I went to everyone looked like me. I graduated from the University of Georgia and went on to earn a master of theology. It was never a matter of if I would go on to college after high school, but where. I have been afforded all the privileges of being white in America. I've never had a hard time accepting that fact; I felt like it was obvious.

Anyone who has studied history knows Europeans colonized the world beginning in the fifteenth century. Our current world system was set up by white men. Therefore, if you are white, you were born into a system that favors those whose ancestors constructed it. Whether you know it, or even agree with it, that is a fact of history. In many ways, if you are white, you've won the genetic lottery. Now what you do with that privilege is another matter, but we definitely have a big head start in life. Some might claim, "My family was never given anything. We had to scratch and fight for everything we built. We had no privilege." That may be true. However, I'm talking about the big picture as we look at history as a whole, which is a much different perspective than looking at a particular family or even one specific generation.

I have three compelling stories that illustrate what I believe to be privilege.

Riding with Birdie Boy

For three years of my twelve-year journey through the US prison industrial complex, I traveled the roads of America with a good friend, Gary Burke, a.k.a. Birdie Boy. We went inside many prisons and schools together as we built the Power of Peace Project. Birdie Boy is an ex-offender who has become a role model to inmates and kids alike. Instead of using his incarceration as an excuse, he has used it as a launching pad to get his master of divinity, and soon he will complete his PhD from a prestigious seminary. He now pastors a church in the heart of Atlanta that helps kids stay off the streets, in school, and out of gangs and prison. He is one of my all-time best friends and one of my heroes. During this stretch where our story begins, I had received credible threats from MS-13, a dangerous international street gang, because of my work with one of their leaders. This will be important as the story continues.

We were on tour in the Northeast with three stops in NYC, Jersey City, and Philadelphia. After a successful trip we were on our way home and happened to be traveling by car in the middle of the night. As we were coming through Virginia, Birdie was driving in my black car, with black-tinted windows, and we both happened to be wearing black. Birdie Boy happens to be a brother of more color and has a beautiful gold tooth, which stands out whenever he flashes that million-dollar smile (gold teeth are a trademark where he is from in South Florida). Birdie likes to drive when we travel, and I'm cool with riding shotgun. He also tends to drive a little fast.

As we traveled along the highway, we suddenly saw blue lights behind us and realized we were being pulled over by a Virginia State Trooper. As the officer came up beside the passenger window, I told Gary not to worry and that I would handle it. I rolled down my window and he asked Birdie to give him his license and proof of insurance. I told him it was my car, so he asked me the same. Then I had a sudden realization, the kind that stops your heart: Birdie is a convicted felon, and we had a problem. But first, a little more back story is needed.

I had been working with a high-profile MS-13 gang leader who was looking at a gang-related murder charge and a potential death-penalty case, as the feds were trying to make an example of him. His gang was enemy number one for the previous administration as well as the current one. MS-13 knew I was working with him, and they sent me a text message to warn me to stop helping him, or they would . . . I can't finish their profane threat, but it was a worst-case scenario for me—and I don't just mean death. So, I went to the gang task force in my city and shared my predicament. They told me in no uncertain terms to do three things: Learn self-defense, follow the task force's directives if I realize I'm being followed, and get a gun, a conceal-and-carry license, and learn how to use it. I did all three.

Back to the story at hand. As the trooper asked me for my license and insurance, the realization hit me that as a convicted felon, Birdie is not permitted to be in the presence of a firearm under any circumstance. This is a revocable violation. I froze. As I stammered, I told the officer I didn't know where it was, which was a lie. It was in the glove compartment, along with my nine-millimeter. He said, "Maybe it's in the glove box."

I said, "Or maybe it's in the trunk." I know that sounds stupid, but it's all I could come up with.

He said, "Open the glove compartment."

I did, and that's when it became a situation. He told me to keep my hands where he could see them and for us to step out of the car as he called for backup. As we leaned against the back of my car, I said to Birdie, "I'm so sorry I got us arrested tonight, bro."

He said, "You didn't get us arrested. You got *me* arrested."

I was heartbroken. I hadn't even thought about the gun on our entire trip. Two more squad cars pulled in behind us, and the trooper approached. He asked if Birdie knew he was a convicted felon. Of course he did. He asked if he knew the firearm was in the glove compartment, and Birdie said he didn't. The trooper told me to tell him a story, and to make it brief.

I said, "I am involved in prison-gang intervention, and I recently received a credible threat from MS-13. Do you know who they are?" He said of course he did. I continued, "The gang task force in my city told me to carry a gun. This one is registered to me, and I have a license for it. I am so sorry it's in the car with my friend, and it is not his fault."

He excused himself to go talk to his superior officer. When he returned, he told us to get back in the car. He took out the clip, put my gun in the trunk, and told me to leave it there until we got back to Atlanta. Then he reached his hand through my window to shake mine and said, "Thank you for what you're doing, sir. Keep up the great work, and have a safe trip." Then they all drove away. They happened to be white, just like me.

I turned to Birdie Boy and said, "We dodged a bullet, bro. I'm just glad we didn't go to jail tonight!"

And he calmly replied, "I'm just glad I got me a white boy."

It was obvious to me there was no way we would have been let go that night if I happened to be black. My whiteness gave me a pass and kept my buddy from going back to jail.

The Crash That Saved My Life

In the summer of 2004 I was at the lowest point of my life. It was three o'clock in the morning and I was driving back from a place I never should have been. I was also blackout drunk. I could hardly see, much less drive, as I tried to make my way back home. I almost got there before I passed out. As it just so happened, I veered to the right and flew off the road into a guard rail. I've been back to this place many times since that fateful night, and this is the only guard rail along that lonely stretch of road. One second earlier and I wouldn't be here anymore. One second later and I'd be a sad story, an unfortunate end to a promising life. But I passed out at just the right time, because God is in the details. I got out, a little banged up, and I looked at my car. The front was smashed, the windshield wipers were wiping, the music was blasting, and the car was obviously undriveable.

As I stood there, rather stunned and in a stupor, a cop car pulled up with his blues on. The officer got out and helped me off the road. He asked for my license, and I complied. What happened next is still hard to understand, much less to explain. He put me in the *front* seat without cuffs, where I quickly passed out again. I'd never been in the front seat of a squad car next to the police computer, and I didn't know anyone who had. But that was where he put me, and that was where I sat. The next thing I knew he was gently waking me up. When I looked up, I realized I was at my mailbox. He let me go and didn't even write me a ticket. He also called a tow for my car, and the next day I got a call from a collision center. I never learned that cop's name, so I can't even thank him for his kindness. For some strange reason I had been given another pass.

Once again, life had given me a ridiculous reminder that the color of my skin makes a big difference in how I am treated by this world. I cannot imagine a scenario where I would have been given such grace if my skin were a darker shade. I am the poster boy for white privilege and the king of second chances.

My Daughter and the Protests

My daughter and I have always had a special relationship. She is our free spirit, our dreamer, and now, a freedom fighter. We are so proud of her, and now she is making her way in the world. When your only daughter goes out on her own, there is a fear only a father can understand. She moved out west to take a job and fell in love with the ocean and the West Coast. Recently she traveled back out there for the summer to reconnect with friends and make some special memories. And then everything changed. The day she stepped off the plane was the day George Floyd died. The protests began and Portland, where she was, became the hot spot. I raised her to fight for what she believes in, but this was different—this was real, as real as it gets. As the protests turned to riots at night, I felt a fear I had never experienced. I couldn't protect her now; this was her fight. Forbidding her to participate was out of the question, now that she was out of the house. All I could do was pray for my little girl out there fighting the good fight in a dangerous world.

So, I called my friend Birdie Boy to get advice and maybe some comfort. He has four daughters who are older than ours, and he

The New Convict Code

is very wise. As I told him about my situation, with fear in my voice, he was so calm, cool, and collected. He always is, and that's one thing I love about him. But this was different. He said, "You got to let her go, bro. Give it to God. She knows where you are, and she knows you are there if she needs you. She'll call you when she does. Now you just gotta trust God and let her go."

That's not what I wanted to hear. And then it struck me. He'd already been through all this. And then it really struck me, and I said, "Birdie, I bet this is what you've felt every day of your life as a black man with daughters."

He replied, "Yes, it is. Welcome to my world, brother." I was reminded again of my special place in this world, which carries very special privileges. My daughter is back on the East Coast and has learned so much from this struggle our country is engaged in. I am so proud of her.

This is my story and not yours. This is my experience, and not necessarily yours, either. You need to come to your own conclusion and have your own conviction about this complex issue we call white privilege. However, I have come to an inescapable conclusion as a white man in America: Things would be very different for me if I were a brother of more color living in the Land of the Free, where "all men are created equal."

Currently, over 40 percent of those incarcerated are African American, though black people account for only 13 percent of the US population. This is a very troubling statistic that we need to take a closer look at. There is a systemic root here that desperately needs to be addressed, but this is a subject that deserves more time than we have here and is beyond the scope of this book. Suffice it to say that I believe white privilege plays a role in this dangerous trend.

The Dreaded Racist Label

We are living in a day and age where more and more labels are created every day to describe people and put them into categories. Once you get tagged with a label, it is difficult to shed. If you are labeled a Republican, some might assume that on some level you must be a racist, until you prove them wrong. If you are labeled as a Black Lives Matter supporter, then some may wrongly assume you are an anarchist or socialist, until they know differently. If you are labeled with a mental illness, then many will assume you are unstable and undependable, unless you can prove them wrong. This is a dangerous trend.

There are two basic types of people in the world: those who are moving forward and living, and those who are moving backward and slowly dying. Some are healthy and vibrant, while others are unhealthy and stunted. We have healthy people and sick people, not simply good people and bad. If we have good people and bad people, then where is the line of demarcation? Who is the last good person, and who is the first bad person? Some of the best men I know are behind the wire, and many dangerous people are still in the free world. I've found that you cannot truly know what's inside a person, and certainly not merely by the label they wear.

We have noble judges and those who are addicts; we have honorable politicians and those who are crooks. We have righteous men and women of the cloth, and we have pedophile priests. So where is the line? I've done some beautiful things in my life, and I've done some terrible things. Am I on the good list at times in my life and then exiled to the bad list during a bad season? And where would I rank on this list of the good, bad, and the ugly? If I compare myself to the worst, then maybe I feel like I'm one of the good guys, until, of course, I make a bad decision.

But there is one label that is almost impossible to shed if you get tagged with it: "racist." We see people go to great lengths to avoid being tagged a racist. I am reminded of a story that made headlines a short time ago. A young white woman was walking her dog in Central Park without a leash. Park rules say you must have your dog on a leash at all times. A black gentleman approached her and reminded her of that rule, which was a responsible thing to do. From what I've read, it sounds like he didn't do it harshly, but the woman was upset about being challenged by a stranger. She demanded that he get away from her, and then she got out her phone and called the police. "There is a black man harassing me! He's scaring me!" All of this was caught on someone else's phone, and it went viral. She offered a vague and general apology, like we see so often on Twitter these days, and then came the comment that took all of her apology away: "However, I'm not a racist."

None of us wants to think of ourselves as a racist. We certainly do not want to be labeled that way for life. However, there is another way her apology could have gone. What if she had said this instead? "I have never believed myself to be a racist. I was not raised that way, and that is not the way I try to live my life. However, something came out of my heart today that shocked and saddened me. I need to take a good, long, hard look at myself and see if there are things that I am unaware of. I prejudged that man, and that is not the way I want to be. I never want to make anyone feel the way I made that man feel, and I am truly sorry. Please forgive me." Genuine humility. If we are gut-level honest, I think we have all thought and said things over the course of our lives that we regret, things that do not reflect our true nature. A bad decision does not make a good person bad. And a good decision does not make a bad person good. Whoops, there I go again with labels. Are there really any good guys and bad guys? I guess it just depends on the day, and it is all relative, anyway.

Chapter Sixteen
A FORGOTTEN CITY REMEMBERED

The Edmund Pettus Bridge in Selma, Alabama

I have always been fascinated with Selma, Alabama. What an important city, one that played such a crucial role in the struggle for civil rights at such a pivotal time in our nation's history. Selma didn't ask for any of it, no more than a young preacher named Dr. Martin Luther King Jr., who got caught up in the movement as a young preacher in Montgomery. When the nation witnessed the brutality of Bloody Sunday on the Edmund Pettus Bridge on March 7, 1965, they could no longer sit idly by and do nothing. It was because they saw beautiful people being beaten mercilessly and enduring brutal, unjust suffering. Do you want to truly inspire a nation that has almost 70 percent of its population claiming Christianity? Then suffer like Jesus did and watch your spectators rally around you. So, Selma firmly carved its place into the civil-rights struggle in America through her courageous and nonviolent stand against brutality.

In 2015, moved by my visit to the Civil Rights Memorial in Montgomery, I decided to walk the same walk as Martin for the fiftieth anniversary of Bloody Sunday. With a small band of young brothers, and myself, we marched those fifty-four miles in two and a half days, and I was forever connected to Selma. When the city council, a couple of pastors, and a few community leaders reached out to me in 2018 because of the work I was doing around youth gang violence, I was humbled and honored to take my work to that historic civil-rights city. I've been going over from Atlanta monthly ever since.

I began with the kids and launched our Protect the Dream program in two of the high schools there. I was shocked by the condition of one of the high schools. It looked like an abandoned elementary school, or maybe a broken-down little church. The kids and staff were beautiful, but I was saddened by the environment in which these kids were trying to learn. I had been invited to begin my work there because of the violence erupting in the tougher areas of town, especially with the youth. When a young man was shot right in the middle of the day downtown, a local businessman decided enough was enough and reached out to me.

I first connected with local pastors, politicians, educators, law enforcement, the Muslim community, and nonprofit organizations. I wanted to understand Selma before I even thought about bringing solutions. How in the world could I help without truly understanding the issues or finding out if the community even wanted my help? I began to learn from a wounded city who has a distrust for outsiders coming to "save Selma." Obviously, they thought I was just another of the same—and maybe I was, but I continued to learn.

News spreads fast in a small town, and soon the word got out that there was a white outsider in town on a regular basis. I was given a new nickname, as they began to call me their "blue-eyed soul brother!" When I met with Muslims, the Christians noticed. When I met with a pastor, the rival preachers noticed. If I did a certain radio interview, those who opposed those folks noticed. When I met with a particular politician, their opponents noticed. At one point I stood in front of the chamber of commerce while doing a presentation and stated, "I am here to learn. I am here to connect. So when you see me meeting with this person or that, or serving with this organization or another, or if I visit this particular church or mosque, please reserve judgment. How can I learn if I don't reach out to all sides? Please don't label me based on my affiliations. Simply watch my life, and you'll be able to tell if I'm for real or not." I am still striving to earn their respect and trust, and for good reason.

My Gift to Martin

After following Dr. King for decades, I was drawn back to Montgomery several years ago to learn more about the civil-rights struggle. I had never been to the memorial there, so I drove over for the day. Throughout the exhibition, the city of Selma was featured, and when I realized it was less than an hour away, I got back in my car and continued driving west. This was my first visit to Selma. As I approached the historic Edmund Pettus Bridge, I was reminded of Bloody Sunday and the heroic courage that men like John Lewis displayed for the cause of voting rights in the Black Belt.

I walked up that bridge over the Alabama River and looked

out over the city. I felt like I was supposed to do something, and so I prayed. The answer I received was to march, so I gathered my sons and a few of their friends and we walked in Martin's steps from Selma all the way to the State Capitol in Montgomery. That drew me even closer to Dr. King, as he has always had quite a pull on my life and work. Three years later community leaders reached out to me from Selma and asked if I would come and help with youth crime and violence prevention. I gladly agreed and decided it would be my gift to Martin. They were shocked when they learned I already had Selma tattooed on my arm.

A Microcosm of America

In many ways, Selma is a microcosm of America today. After all the important changes that came for people of color because of the heroic men and women who gave their lives for the struggle, the city is still much the same as it was then. Like many small towns and cities across our nation, Selma remains divided racially, economically, politically, and religiously. Although laws were changed, the hearts of men remain the same—stuck in a state of divide. When people learn that I am doing work there, invariably they say something about the civil-rights history, and they're shocked to learn that this iconic city still has many of the same issues it faced in 1965, just like many communities across America.

The citizens of Selma are beautiful people who love their city, and they don't deserve the way the nation has treated them. Every year when the anniversary of Bloody Sunday comes back around, important people show up and walk across that iconic bridge. They make grand speeches and get their photo op, and shout things like, "Remember Selma!" and "We will never forget!" Then they get in their cars and travel back across that bridge only to forget the people there once again.

I faced much of the same skepticism and mistrust when I began going over to Selma. Outsiders stand out, and I am hard to miss. I spent a whole year trying to build relationships and win Selmians' respect and trust. Years of prison ministry had taught me this is a ministry of *showing up*, and that what you do shouts so loud that sometimes people can't hear what you say. So, I continued showing up.

I also learned I didn't have the solutions or even know what the issues were without walking and talking with Selmians. They have had so many people come from other parts of the country with their own agendas, promising to help. I was just another one of those users, as far as they were concerned. Why should they think any differently? So, I decided I would ask questions and learn, and then ask more questions and learn some more. A wise man who has been in politics for years in Alabama told me not to make the same mistake most people make when coming to serve Selma. He said, "If you're coming here to save us, then you're automatically putting yourself in a superior position to us. If you think we need saving, and that you're the one who can do it, then that must mean you think you're better than us before you even get here." He was right, and I committed that I would not make that mistake.

You see, the brothers behind the wire had taught me that very lesson over the years. There was no way I was going in there to try to save them, and I did not consider myself better than them, not even for a day. I would even tell them, "I'm not coming here to bring God to you, but rather to find God in you, because I know He is there." I set out to use the same approach with the beautiful residents of Selma. I'm not trying to save them; I am coming to find the beauty in this city and shout it from the rooftops. Maybe one day they'll accept me as one of their own. That would make me prouder than you could imagine. Maybe one day they'll make me an honorary Selmian, just as the brothers behind the wire eventually accepted me as one of their own.

Shining Light in a Dark Place

A natural place to continue my work in Selma was at the county jail. The sheriff of Dallas County is respected by his community. He was relatively new to this position in Selma, though not new to being a sheriff. He has experience and a great reputation in his field, and we established a good working relationship quickly. I believe he wants the best for the people under his charge.

The jail just outside of Selma is different than many I've experienced, and it has serious issues that need to be resolved. I know the sheriff has made significant changes and is working to bring about peace in Selma.

I write this section for the beautiful people of Selma who have loved ones who are being arrested or detained, which is very hard on a family. I share these things respectfully in the hopes that things will continue to change and that brothers and sisters behind the wire will be treated with dignity and respect in a place where no one wants to be.

On my first visit to the jail, I noticed very little security. I was not wanded or frisked, I wasn't asked if I had any contraband, and I didn't walk through a metal detector. Once inside, I saw conditions that broke my heart. Many of the brothers live in the old part of the jail where it is dark and dreary. Several told me they hadn't seen or heard from their attorney in months. One brother said he hadn't seen the sun in three years (whether that is true or not, it had obviously been a very long time). There's a recreation yard and a basketball court that hadn't been used for as long as the brothers could remember. There were no county-issued uniforms or shoes—at least I didn't see any—and the food was substandard at best.

I went to talk to a brother in solitary confinement. The cell was pitch black, and this man had to get on his knees to peer through a small slot in the door to see me and talk to me as he crouched in complete darkness. I asked why his lights weren't on, and I was told it was because they weren't working.

In the toughest prisons, the brothers get time outside to see the sun and get some fresh air, even if it's only for an hour in a cage. Even death-row inmates get their time outside, which is their right. There were changes made with the staff and leadership at the jail, and things are improving there as we speak, which gives me hope. There are similar things going on in facilities across the country, which is easy to get away with because very few from the outside ever see it, and there is little oversight or accountability. It's time to shine light on a dark place.

While inside, I quickly found out who the men of influence were. It was quite easy to build a friendship, and then one of my new friends began to educate me on the "other side" of Selma. Winning his trust was key, as news travels fast when there are only 150 brothers in there. The sheriff allowed me to go to every cell and introduce myself and encourage the brothers. We brought donuts in on Mondays, which they were very grateful for. We began the Forty Days to Freedom with twelve influential brothers who represented different areas of Selma. Before long, there was a buzz, and everybody wanted in on this "peace thing."

Then I made an offer to the guys. I said, "Go tell your people about me and have them invite me into your homes. I would love to meet your families, break bread, and tell them about the hope we have for their sons, brothers, and fathers."

They were surprised. "You want to go to *our* neighborhoods?" This is one method to connect with underserved communities: Serve at the jail and build relationships with the brothers who have the most influence, and then have them vouch for me with their families. These brothers in the local jails have connections on the streets and influence with the young people who are lining up to get in.

One of my friends at this jail, who is a brother of influence, grew up in a housing project in Selma called GWC Homes (George Washington Carver). This is one of the areas where a lot of the crime and violence has been happening. Beautiful families live there, but generational poverty has taken its toll. Kids are growing up there with little to no hope of ever breaking out of this perpetual cycle. How do we engage these kids who are so difficult to reach? We change the hearts and minds of their big brothers, uncles, and fathers. They might be the only ones these kids will listen to, and they are the antivirus they need from brothers who have been inoculated by those same tough streets.

Pastors on the Front Lines

I was originally invited to Selma by a brother named Bob Frazer who arranged for me to meet with members of the city council, local business leaders, and several pastors. Bob has become a good friend to me. Three of the people I met with that day have become trusted advisors and confidants. Two are pastors; one is black, one is white, and they are partners in the Gospel. The third is a basketball coach, mentor, and teacher. He happens to be Muslim, and I respect his faith, his walk with God, and the example he sets for the kids. These brothers teach me about a community that I do not know. They are invaluable.

Pastor John Grayson is one of the most respected people in Selma. In a town where there are many rivals and much divide,

The New Convict Code

like many small communities around our country, it is rare to find someone whom everybody, and I mean everybody, speaks well of. I've never known a pastor—and I've known many—who tirelessly serves his community as much as this man. His church literally feeds thousands of meals to families every month. We took some kids from Atlanta over to serve, and we were amazed to see all the hungry families who showed up. They don't just get a meal, but a whole basket full of groceries. I treasure the time we spend together, and I so value the advice he gives me. His congregation, the Gospel Tabernacle, has graciously adopted me and even made me an honorary member! Pastor Grayson has ministered to me when I was discouraged, and given me advice when I didn't know the next right move, and for that I am truly grateful.

Another mentor is Pastor Steve Burton. Early on, when I was trying to build relationships with influencers and community leaders, everyone kept directing me to Pastor Burton. I was impressed when I learned of his huge heart for missions. Steve has served in Belfast, Ireland, consistently over the years in some dangerous areas during some dangerous times, and he continues to support those beautiful people to this day.

What I love about Pastor Burton is how real and authentic he is. He's not over-religious, like many prominent preachers, but rather deeply spiritual. In a world where people are guarded, especially with newcomers and outsiders, Pastor Burton has opened his life to me. He's the kind of brother that if you don't want the truth, don't ask him the question. He teaches me the inner workings of a city with a deep, rich history, but also complex issues and strong personalities. I trust his wisdom and advice.

Whenever I go to Selma each month, I make sure to book time with both of these dear brothers. They help me understand the dynamics and personalities of this fascinating community so that I continue to make the right moves. Sometimes I'll think something is a great idea, until Pastors Grayson and Burton show me otherwise.

Selma has over a hundred churches in a city of eighteen thousand people. There is no way to effectively heal Selma without bringing the spiritual leaders together. A Selmian once told me, "If you can bring the pastors together in Selma, then you will have done something that has never been done before." If Dr. King were still alive today, I believe he would have started there. Just like he did in his famous "Letter from a Birmingham Jail," he would call out the pastors and challenge them to use their voices, collectively, to heal a wounded community. If the people of God can come together in Selma and in other communities across America, we could start a spiritual revival that would be impossible to contain. But once again, this takes humility, which is becoming more and more rare with leaders in today's politicized climate.

I also want to show some love to my brother and friend Coach Ronald Lane. He was the first friend I made in Selma as we worked together with his Selma High School basketball team. He loves the kids so much, and tirelessly mentors them and tries to keep them in school and off the streets. He welcomed me into his family and introduced me to his community. He vouched for me before anyone ever knew who I was. We are soul brothers for life.

These three brothers are invaluable to my work. They are much more than just friends; they are my advisors, my comrades, my counselors, my consiglieres, and my partners in the faith. Selma wouldn't accept me without brothers like these standing up for me. I pray that you have wise teachers in your life too. Brothers in arms fighting a common battle. That's the good stuff.

Coach Lane with His Selma POPP Squad

A Pair of Unlikely Friends

I was invited to a men's Bible study by one of my new friends in Selma, and I quickly accepted the invitation. It turns out this invitation would introduce me to a side of Selma I had yet to meet. These were the sons of third-generation white Selmians, a side I definitely needed to understand in order to understand Selma as a whole. Many of these men grew up at the Selma Country Club, which has been around for 123 years.

The first thing that impressed me was the book this all-white Bible study group was going through together. It was about racial unity and prejudice. There was also a brother of color in the group who had been attending recently, which had never happened before with this fellowship. Add to that one of the white brothers who was there had recently gotten caught up in a racial situation in Selma, and the table was set for a fascinating evening.

A couple of months earlier, a white man had been shot by a young black man as he was jogging through town in the middle of the morning. This happened right when violent protests around racism and police brutality were beginning in several major American cities. There were rumors that the country club might be burned down, as parts of many other American cities were set on fire, but nothing ever materialized. The brother who had been shot was at the Bible study this night. He ended up being in the hospital for two weeks after the shooting but made a full recovery. I was moved as he shared his story that evening. He spoke of how it felt lying in that hospital bed not knowing what to do or how to respond. I tried to imagine how I would have reacted if I went for a jog one morning and was gunned down by a brother of color in a passing car simply because I happened to be white.

Here's how this white brother decided to respond to this attack. First of all, he said he understood that the young shooter had mental-health issues and needed forgiveness, which he gladly gave. Then he told us about his decision to model forgiveness to his hometown. Keep in mind that Selma has a population of only eighteen thousand, so everybody knows everybody else's business. After his two-week recovery in the hospital, he decided he would get his hair cut at a local black barber shop while he was still in a wheelchair. He talked of his fear of going there, and not knowing how he would be received. He asked his pregnant wife, and she said she wouldn't feel good about it unless she went with him. So that's what they did. Then he shared about how he was so encouraged by the way they were treated with kindness and respect.

I doubt I would have even had that thought, much less carried it out. I told him in front of the group how I was inspired by his heart and willingness to forgive and embrace the other, especially in these times. Many on opposing sides of these complex issues are unwilling to forgive the other even though they weren't personally involved in the events they so adamantly oppose. I was moved.

Then our new visitor, a brother of color, began to share about his unique experience. He talked about his life and specifically about his conversion. He grew up in Selma, and shared with humility that he had always hated white people because of how they had treated him. He said he had never met any good white people and he believed they were "white devils," as Malcolm had called Caucasians in the sixties.

He spoke of getting more and more depressed and angry, even to the point of being suicidal. He became so upset that he got a gun and made a decision. He said, "The next white person who disrespects me is going to die." And he meant it. So, he carried a gun and waited to see who it would be. On a sidenote, we should all remember that whenever we decide to disrespect someone, they might very well be on their last day too.

As he walked along the street one night, he passed a church. He felt as though the Spirit of God was telling him to go into that church, but he ignored it and kept walking. The Spirit wouldn't let him go, so he finally turned around. As he entered the lobby, a tiny white lady stepped out and hugged him. She wouldn't let him go, and then she said, "Hug me back!" He wouldn't do it because he was afraid someone might see a large black man hugging a little white lady and get him in big trouble. But she wouldn't let go, so he hugged her back. He couldn't explain what happened next, but something changed in him. He shared that what he needed was to meet a really good white person, and he finally met one. God healed him from that moment forward, and he's never been the same. He said he has never stopped going to that white church and attends to this day.

Here was an interesting twist to the story. That white woman ended up leaving the church after she got mad at God. She felt like He had let her down, so she just left. Guess who has been pursuing her ever since? That's right, her new friend and brother.

He goes by her work and says, "You think you're gonna bring me to God and then run away from Him? Oh, no, you're not!" He goes by her house and says, "You're gonna bring me to church and then leave it? Not on my watch!" I love that story.

These two brothers living in a small rural city in the Black Belt, fighting the same issues of systemic racism and police brutality, have found the answer: Embrace your enemy, make them your friend, and model compassion and forgiveness to your community.

It's Time to Remember Selma

I don't believe it was intentional, but somewhere along the way, Selma was forgotten. She played such an important role in the civil-rights struggle and suffered, even bled, for the cause. However, as the nation's attention turned to the eruption of violence after Dr. King was assassinated, the eyes of our country never really turned back. Out of sight, out of mind. It's time to remember her once again, and not just on the anniversary of Bloody Sunday. One could make a strong case that Selma has been used to promote the message of equality for others, while still being victimized through inequality. If there is a city in the country that deserves some love, it is Selma. Businesses have left, civil-rights organizations have bigger priorities, and she continues to suffer. What will it take to remember her and rebuild the town that Dr. King and others cared about so much? I, for one, will continue to serve her and try to inspire others to do the same.

We have taken several groups of students on trips to Selma to teach young people their history and learn from our past mistakes in the hope that their generation will not make the same ones. You should see their minds come alive as they learn about Selma's rich civil-rights history, walk across that iconic bridge, and tour the Voting Rights Museum. I would like to think that the POPP kids who have spent time there are seeing all that is going on in our nation around racism and police brutality through a slightly different lens. We can't expect this young generation to know things we have not taught them or modeled for them. How can they know if they don't go? They are so impressionable, so let us give them some new impressions.

Just imagine if the nation truly remembered Selma again. What if we showed her love and helped her come alive and become "our beloved community," as Dr. King spoke of? She would become a shining light to other wounded communities across the nation who need hope. As a Selmian once told me, "If it happens here, it can happen anywhere." Let it be so.

The Dysfunctional Triangle

I was working in a prison in Ellsworth, Kansas, several years ago, and I stumbled upon something that changed my perspective. In small towns like Ellsworth, prisons are typically the biggest employer in the area. They employ hundreds of local residents, and all those people have kids who go to schools, and many are connected to different churches there. In a small town, news travels fast. So, word got out during the second phase of POPP that there was a program going on at the prison that was turning tough prisoners into peacemakers and positive role models. When local schools heard about our work, I began to be invited to speak at student assemblies. I love working with kids, so I gladly accepted.

I told the kids stories about these hated, feared, and forgotten men who were now becoming role models to kids in the free world. I had been promising the brothers behind the wire that they would become role models, and now it was happening. The kids were spellbound because it was real, live, gangster hip-hop, which is their world. The teachers and staff were amazed that the kids were so well behaved, and I just smiled.

Then I began going back to the prisoners and telling them that kids were following their example and not to let them down. Then, of course, I went back to the kids and told them those brothers behind the wire were literally putting their lives on the line for them and not to let *them* down. A cool symbiotic relationship was developing. Before long, I asked the principal if they would like for me to take the kids through a phase of POPP. They were ecstatic. So, we ran our POPP program at the prison while running POPP in one of the local middle schools at the same time.

Good news travels fast, so it wasn't long before I got a call from a local pastor inquiring about what was going on in the prisons and schools. We got the church to join the inmates and the students, and to blanket both projects with prayer. It was a thing of beauty as inmates, students, and congregants went through different versions of the forty-day POPP programs together. That gave rise to what I call the Dysfunctional Triangle.

In every community, large or small, you will surely find three institutions: jails, schools, and churches. The problem is that these three institutions are oftentimes dysfunctional. The schools have become a pipeline to the prisons. The prisons are releasing men who are more violent than when they went in. And the churches often are sitting on their hands and preaching to the converted. Unless we heal these three institutions, our communities will never truly thrive.

So, I went to work on a process where all three can unite in common programs, designed just for them, and together heal their wounded community from the inside out. The inmates become role models to the kids, the kids become role models to each other, and the churches serve the least of these, which is the heart of Jesus. And they all do it together, forty days at a time. The inmates go through one of my books called *Forty Days to Freedom: Breaking the Chains That Bind Us*. The students go through one of my books called *Protect the Dream: 40 Days of Power*. And the congregants go through a third book of mine called *Forty Days of Prayer: Seven Steps to a Spiritual Breakthrough*.

This is my plan to bring wounded communities together that are being torn apart by recent events in our country. There is no downside to this process. The inmates find purpose and self-esteem, the students find unlikely role models and inspiration, and the churches find a new spiritual fire as they serve those less fortunate. It is a true win-win-win. Ellsworth, Kansas, was the first time I experimented with this new approach, and I was encouraged once again.

POPP Brothers at Ellsworth Take the Peace Pledge

Conclusion

Happy, Joyous, and Free at Last

I've seen too much to believe mine is an impossible dream. I've seen it work in maximum-security prisons, and I've seen it work in women's penitentiaries. I've seen it work in juvenile prisons, and I've seen it work in rehab centers. I've seen it work with Crips, Bloods, Gangster Disciples, the Aryan Brotherhood, Militant Muslims, Latin Kings, MS-13, and even cartel members. You can't tell me it won't work on the streets, because I've seen it work there too. I've witnessed it work in tough inner-city schools and rich suburban schools, and I've seen it work in churches as well. We are built for peace, and we all yearn for it. We just need a big enough *why*.

I've seen so much evidence of positive change, and witnessed so many powerful transformations, that I have become ridiculously confident in these proposed solutions. Just give us six months in whichever prison you choose, anywhere in the country. Give us access to the right leaders and the space to meet with them regularly. We will take one hundred men at a time through three phases of POPP over that six-month period, and here is my promise: In 180 days, we will have a living, breathing peace movement and a functional, effective peace council. I guarantee you that violence will decrease. Do you believe me? Try me, I dare you. I believe because I've seen too much to be skeptical or cynical any longer.

Those whom the world rejects, disregards, dismisses, marginalizes, judges, hates, fears, and blames are the ones God chose to change this fallen preacher's life. I'll close with a powerful story about the *least* of the least of these.

Redemption on Death Row

When you hear the words "death row," your energy shifts and you begin to wonder what those who live there might have done. We all know that in order to get a death sentence, the crime has to be particularly cruel and violent. So, we see death-row inmates as the worst of the worst, pure evil. I've had the opportunity to work on death row in Alabama and Louisiana several times, and it changed my perspective. Wherever you stand on the death-penalty issue, it becomes much more difficult when you get to know men on the row. They become real people with real stories. They have families, and each has a unique journey that led them to whatever happened on that fateful day when they did the unthinkable.

I have visited with many men on death row, and I have become friends with a number of them. I have lost three of my friends to capital punishment, and I have more friends still waiting—waiting on a call they hope will never come. I have gifts from them in my office: a beautiful jewelry box made by a friend named Donald who is still living on the row in Alabama, and a painting that hangs on my wall that was painted by a man named Michael on that same row, who we lost in 2019. When you get close enough to these men, you see their humanity, as broken as it might be.

One of the men I came to know was David, who received his death penalty as a young man. He was on death row for over twenty years, and they took him in 2019 at the age of forty-six. By all accounts David was a hard young man when he came in, angry and defiant. He kept to himself and cared little for the other inmates. In this particular prison, these men get fairly regular time together as a group and have become a kind of fraternity, as they are all headed to the same destination. They have little to envy. His brothers on the row told me all about his transformation.

Over the years, David began to change. Spending time with other men, rather than in isolation, can have that effect, and little by little he softened up. A few brothers have become spiritual leaders to the others, and many of them have developed true faith. They have learned to depend on one another, and they help each other with their struggles. I have seen them mourn and grieve over the loss of their brothers when the state takes another one of them. David became one of these men who cared about his comrades. He would help the others when he could, and he began to learn the Bible and the power of true fellowship.

When I met him, and during the subsequent times I saw him, he was gentle and humble in spirit, even kind. But the brothers told me he hadn't always been like that, that he used to be a completely different person. However, people can change, and that's what he did. One day he got the call—it was his time. I can't imagine what that feels like. Not knowing when your time will come, and then after a simple phone call you know the exact time of your death. How would that change me if I knew the month, the day, and the hour of my transition? We can really never know how it feels, but David does.

He was scheduled to be executed at 7:00 p.m. on an evening I was to give a speech. My presentation began at 7:00 p.m. as well. I had the strangest feeling as I began my introductory remarks, knowing my friend was being strapped to the gurney. The spectators were filing into the viewing room behind the glass, and the curtain was opened as my audience took their seats as well. I had a hard time keeping my mind on my task, and I probably didn't do the best job for my clients that night. I wondered what David was feeling and how he was reacting. Many men lose it and freak out, which is understandable. Many have a prepared statement. Others are hard and refuse to speak or look at anyone in the viewing room. But David was different. He had spent years preparing for this moment.

A friend of mine who has been serving on this particular death row for the last thirty years was present at the execution and recounted to me how the evening unfolded. As the warden walked into the room that was filled with an eerie silence, he turned and looked at my friend. The warden had probably seen many different responses over the years, but I'm not sure he had ever seen what he was about to witness. David looked at him and smiled. Then he said softly to the warden, "It's okay, sir. Everything will be all right." They asked him if he had any final words, and he simply said, "I trust Jesus with my soul." Then they flipped the switches that release the toxic cocktail, and David went to sleep.

Imagine the faith it would take to handle the moment of your death like that when you've been fearing it for over twenty years. Imagine the feelings and thoughts that would be racing through your mind. To have the kind of peace he displayed would take years of soul work and self-reflection. I will never discount or excuse the things he did or the lives he destroyed; I only know that he changed me. As crazy as it seems, a hated, feared, and forgotten death-row convict showed me how to die. One thing I know: Whenever I pass, I want it to be an honorable death. Maybe God allowed me to witness one in an unexpected place.

That is the story of my life. God has allowed this knucklehead to see some of His most amazing work in places no one is looking. But He has given me this charge: "Go and tell the world about what you have seen and heard." Sounds like that original charge my pastor gave me, doesn't it? *Go find out what God is up to and come back and tell us.* I will continue to do just that, and hope somebody is listening. I'm so glad God loves knuckleheads.

Final Thoughts from Sir Brown

Many times along this journey, I've been approached or stopped by an OG, a clergyman, a counselor, a deputy warden, or warden, and asked to share a part of my mind with someone who is mentally traveling in the wrong direction. Sometimes it's an individual, but oftentimes it's a group. I love giving credit to the people who have mentored me. But for this particular request, I instantly recall words from two of my mentors in Jersey City.

Rasheed says, "If you're the smartest person in your group, find another group."

My friend Alim says, "Be selective. Be selective in the thoughts you have, the words you speak, what you watch, what you listen to, the foods you eat, and what you drink." He says, "Be selective in your style of dress, the mate you choose to associate with, and the material you read." He says, *"Be selective in the people you borrow from and the ones you lend to."*

Be selective. Only two words, but for me they are profound. Be selective. And that is how I live my life on the chain gang, and the way I'll live it when they send me back into the free world. The state says I'll never go home, but I refuse to believe that. I answer to a different authority, and I'll leave it up to Him. Peace to you and yours from the brothers behind the wire.

—Sir Brown

To My Brothers Behind the Wire

I am forever grateful; you saved my life. You taught me to keep my word, because you live in a place where you must. You taught me to show respect, because you live in a place where you'd better. You taught me to be loyal to my friends, because you live in a place where you need someone you can count on. You taught me true courage, because you live in a place where you have to take a stand. You taught me to never give up, because you live in a place where quitting isn't an option. You helped me find my heart again, and I will never forget that. I will continue to fight for you to be free—I feel as though I owe you that. I'll see you in the free world someday. Until then, be the heroes we've been waiting for. You *are* the Power of Peace.

Acknowledgments

All my love to my mother and stepfather, who have been by my side every step of the way. To my wife and kids, who have been so patient and supportive as I traveled far and wide and spent so much time on the road following this dream. To my Uncle Kit who is my role model, consigliere, and namesake. To my board of directors, who have protected me and provided invaluable advice and wise counsel. To my publishing family at BookLogix for helping me get my message to the world. To all the wardens, principals, coaches, and pastors who have trusted me with their residents, students, players, and congregants. To my dad, who I miss every day of my life. And finally, to all my brothers and sisters behind the wire who have changed my life forever and helped me find my noble purpose and my grand obsession. I am forever grateful to all of you. Peace to you and yours.

Bibliography

Alper, Mariel, and Matthew R. Durose. *2018 Update on Prisoner Recidivism: A 9-Year Follow-up Period (2005–2014)*. US Department of Justice, Bureau of Justice Statistics (May 2018). https://www.bjs.gov/content/pub/pdf/18upr9yfup0514.pdf.

American Civil Liberties Union. "Mass Incarceration." ACLU.org. Accessed November 6, 2020.
https://www.aclu.org/issues/smart-justice/mass-incarceration.

Barone, Emily. "The Wrongly Convicted: Why more falsely accused people are being exonerated today than ever before." From *TIME Innocent: The Fight Against Wrongful Convictions*, February 17, 2017. https://time.com/wrongly-convicted/.

Benns, Whitney. "American Slavery, Reinvented." *The Atlantic*. September 21, 2015.
https://www.theatlantic.com/business/archive/2015/09/prison-labor-in-america/406177/.

Bureau of Justice Statistics. *Prisoners 1925–81*. US Department of Justice. December 1982.
https://www.bjs.gov/content/pub/pdf/p2581.pdf.

Clarke, Matt. "Long-Term Recidivism Studies Show High Arrest Rates." *Prison Legal News*. May 3, 2019.
https://www.prisonlegalnews.org/news/2019/may/3/long-term-recidivism-studies-show-high-arrest-rates/.

Cohen, Michael. "How for-profit prisons have become the biggest lobby no one is talking about." *Washington Post*. April 28, 2015. https://www.washingtonpost.com/posteverything/wp/2015/04/28/how-for-profit-prisons-have-become-the-biggest-lobby-no-one-is-talking-about/.

Collier, Lorna. "Incarceration Nation." *American Psychological Association* 45, no. 9 (October 2014): 56. Accessible online at https://www.apa.org/monitor/2014/10/incarceration.

Cooper, Amy. "Statement from Amy Cooper on Central Park Incident." PR Newswire. May 26, 2020. https://www.prnewswire.com/news-releases/statement-from-amy-cooper-on-central-park-incident-301065492.html.

Criminal: How Lockup Quotas and "Low-Crime Taxes" Guarantee Profits for Private Prison Corporations. Washington, DC: In the Public Interest, 2013. http://www.njjn.org/uploads/digital-library/Criminal-Lockup-Quota,-In-the-Public-Interest,-9.13.pdf.

Decker, Charles. "Time to Reckon with Prison Labor." Yale University Institution for Social and Policy Studies. Accessed November 6, 2020. https://isps.yale.edu/news/blog/2013/10/time-to-reckon-with-prison-labor-0.

Durocher, Christopher Wright. "The Rise of Plea Bargains and Fall of the Right to Trial." American Constitution Society. April 4, 2018. https://www.acslaw.org/expertforum/the-rise-of-plea-bargains-and-fall-of-the-right-to-trial/.

ExcelinEd. "Does K-3 reading matter? Ask the 70% of inmates who can't read." The Foundation for Excellence in Education. March 28, 2016. https://www.excelined.org/edfly-blog/does-k-3-reading-matter-ask-the-70-of-inmates-who-cant-read/.

Hager, Eli. "A Mass Incarceration Mystery." *The Marshall Project*. December 15, 2017. https://www.themarshallproject.org/2017/12/15/a-mass-incarceration-mystery.

Herman, Christine. "Most Inmates with Mental Illness Still Wait for Decent Care." NPR.org. February 3, 2019. https://www.npr.org/sections/health-shots/2019/02/03/690872394/most-inmates-with-mental-illness-still-wait-for-decent-care.

Ingraham, Christopher. "Thousands of federal defendants offer help to help the government each year. Trump says that 'almost ought to be outlawed.'" *Washington Post*. August 23, 2018. https://www.washingtonpost.com/business/2018/08/23/thousands-federal-defendants-offer-help-government-each-year-trump-says-practice-almost-ought-be-outlawed/.

Lee, Michelle Ye Hee. "Does the United States really have 5 percent of the world's population and one quarter of the world's prisoners?" *Washington Post*. April 30, 2015. https://www.washingtonpost.com/news/fact-checker/wp/2015/04/30/does-the-united-states-really-have-five-percent-of-worlds-population-and-one-quarter-of-the-worlds-prisoners/.

Lewis, Nicole, and Beatrix Lockwood. "The Hidden Cost of Incarceration." *The Marshall Project*. December 17, 2019. https://www.themarshallproject.org/2019/12/17/the-hidden-cost-of-incarceration.

Lyon, Ed. "Imprisoning America's Mentally Ill." *Prison Legal News*. February 4, 2019. https://www.prisonlegalnews.org/news/2019/feb/4/imprisoning-americas-mentally-ill/.

McGlothlin, David. "Arizona tops in guaranteeing private prisons new customers." Justice Policy Institute. February 18, 2016. (Originally published in *Arizona Sonora News*.) http://www.justicepolicy.org/news/10144.

National Institute on Drug Abuse. "Fentanyl." National Institutes of Health. Accessed November 6, 2020.
https://www.drugabuse.gov/drug-topics/fentanyl.

Partnership Staff. "National Study: Teen Misuse and Abuse of Prescription Drugs Up 33 Percent Since 2008, Stimulants Contributing to Sustained Rx Epidemic." Partnership to End Addiction. April 2013. https://drugfree.org/newsroom/news-item/national-study-teen-misuse-and-abuse-of-prescription-drugs-up-33-percent-since-2008-stimulants-contributing-to-sustained-rx-epidemic/.

Sakala, Leah. "Breaking Down Mass Incarceration in the 2010 Census: State-by-State Incarceration Rates by Race/Ethnicity." Prison Policy Initiative. May 28, 2014.
https://www.prisonpolicy.org/reports/rates.html.

Sawyer, Wendy. Appendix to "How much do incarcerated people earn in each state?" Prison Policy Initiative. April 10, 2017. https://www.prisonpolicy.org/reports/wage_policies.html.

"Youth Confinement: The Whole Pie 2019." Prison Policy Initiative. December 19, 2019.
https://www.prisonpolicy.org/reports/youth2019.html.

Sentencing Project Staff. "Private Prisons in the United States." The Sentencing Project. October 24, 2019.
https://www.sentencingproject.org/publications/private-prisons-united-states/#:~:text=Data%20compiled%20by%20the%20Bureau,of%20America)%2C%20and%20Management%20and.

Statista Research Department. "U.S. capital punishment – time elapsed between sentencing and execution 1990–2018." Statista. October 28, 2020.
https://www.statista.com/statistics/199026/average-time-between-sentencing-and-execution-of-inmates-on-death-row-in-the-us/.

Study International: "More money goes into the US prison system than it does on education." Sept. 16, 2019. https://tinyurl.com/y6lw36ck.

United States Drug Enforcement Administration. "Fentanyl." DEA.gov. Accessed November 6, 2020.
https://www.dea.gov/factsheets/fentanyl.

Wagner, Peter, and Daniel Kopf. "The Racial Geography of Mass Incarceration." Prison Policy Initiative. July 2015. https://www.prisonpolicy.org/racialgeography/report.html.

Walker, Jason Renard. "Unpaid Labor in Texas Prisons Is Modern-Day Slavery." *Truthout*. September 6, 2016.
https://truthout.org/articles/unpaid-labor-in-texas-prisons-is-modern-day-slavery/.

Yahr, Emily. "Yes, prisoners used to sew lingerie for Victoria's Secret – just like in 'Orange Is the New Black' Season 3." *Washington Post*. June 17, 2015.
https://www.washingtonpost.com/news/arts-and-entertainment/wp/2015/06/17/yes-prisoners-used-to-sew-lingerie-for-victorias-secret-just-like-in-orange-is-the-new-black-season-3/.

Yoffe, Emily. "Innocence Is Irrelevant." *The Atlantic*, September 2017. https://www.theatlantic.com/magazine/archive/2017/09/innocence-is-irrelevant/534171/.

About the Author

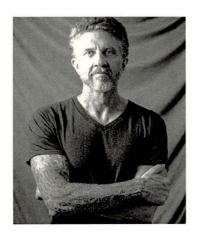

In 2010, Kit Cummings founded the Power of Peace Project. Using the experience he gained resolving conflict in some of the most dangerous areas in the world, he applies his principles to bring about change in prisons, schools, corporations, and the faith-based community. On MLK Day 2020, Kit was recognized by the NAACP, receiving their *Living the Dream Award* for his contribution to civil rights and his work with at-risk youth and prison reform. He was appointed to the Georgia House of Representatives Committee on Youth Gangs and Violence Prevention in 2019, as part of Governor Kemp's initiative to reform prisons and eliminate youth gang violence.

Kit has worked with the incarcerated in over a hundred prisons, jails, detention centers, and rehab facilities and served over ten thousand prisoners. He has journeyed on tours through Africa, Asia, Europe, and Latin America, and has negotiated peace between some of the most notorious gangs inside the US prison system. He delivered an address at the Gandhi Global Peace Summit in Durban, South Africa, to representatives from the Gandhi, King, and Mandela families, as well as other iconic peacemakers from around the world. Kit has taken his Forty Days to Freedom program into La Mesa prison in Tijuana, Mexico, to work with men who are striving to be free, as well as working with addicts and at-risk youth in some of the toughest areas of that war-torn border city. Kit has planted seeds of peace all around the world.

Kit has authored five books, including the award-winning *Peace Behind the Wire: A Nonviolent Resolution*, which has been endorsed by the King Center in Atlanta, GA. The Power of Peace Project interrupts and redirects young people who are on a perilous course and sets them firmly on the pathway to extraordinary dreams.